Praise for *Leaving Johnny Behind*

"*Leaving Johnny Behind* is a remarkable book about the difference between reality and possibility when it comes to helping at-risk readers. Anthony Pedriana, an experienced teacher and administrator, decries the unnecessary casualties of inappropriate literacy instruction. He rightly attributes this state of affairs to the absence of training required of school personnel on the research and practice of effective instruction. He is outraged that in a thirty-year career, he never was taught the consensus findings of multiple research endeavors aimed at solving the reading puzzle. Pedriana's enlightenment began after one teacher showed him that most kids could learn to read well if direct, comprehensive methods were used, and he was willing to follow her lead. Subsequently, Pedriana has, on his own initiative, mined the archives of research and assembled an unusually lucid, accurate, and hard-hitting plea to do better by the kids who depend on us. He gives 'reform' a new meaning: The assurance that all administrators and teachers will be educated before they educate others in reading and literacy. This is a goal worthy of pursuit." —**Louisa C. Moats, Ed.D**, director, Professional Development and Research, Sopris West Educational Services; president, Moats Associates Consulting, Inc.

"*Leaving Johnny Behind* is a gift to anyone who desires to understand why so many of our most vulnerable citizens—our children—struggle to learn to read, and why we, as a country, have let them down." —**Dr. G. Reid Lyon**, former branch chief, National Institute of Child Health and Human Development

"Pedriana has written an important book. Refusing to become embroiled in dichotomous debates, he takes the novel approach of drawing extensively from the best evidence available. The result is a magnificent book that advocates for teachers, good research, and—most of all—student learning. I highly recommend this book for anyone concerned about why we in America don't do a better job educating our children, and what we can do to improve." —**Dr. Jeff Lucas**, associate professor and director of graduate studies, Department of Sociology, University of Maryland

"As an elementary school principal puzzled by the poor results of his school's reading programs, Pedriana is to be congratulated for taking the time to investigate carefully the research on beginning reading instruction. His effort serves as a model to other elementary school principals and to those who train them. And the conclusions he reached should serve as a call to arms: low-performing schools often perform so poorly *because of, not despite*, the pedagogical training their reading teachers have received." —**Sandra Stotsky**, 21st Century Chair in Teacher Quality, University of Arkansas

"Pedriana's outstanding book should be required reading for every superintendent, principal and teacher at all levels, and a central text in every school of education." —**Janet Stratton**, president, founder, The Reading Institute, Williamstown, Massachusetts

"Pedriana's book, *Leaving Johnny Behind*, is a gift to all teachers, administrators, and parents who care that *ALL* children become successful at the first and most important job of their lives: learning to read. His elegant summary of research clarifies five decades of reading research, identifying best practices and key ideas in literacy instruction. His honest examination of literacy practices that work and don't work will sharpen the eyes and minds of all those who look to have best literacy practices in their own schools. This book maps the path to equity and opportunity that is the promise of a literate society." —**Carolyn Olivier**, former education director, Ennis William Cosby Foundation and co-founder of Landmark College, Putney, Vermont

"Every parent, school board member, and policy maker in America should read this story to understand the incredible challenges of implementing evidence-based reading programs that work in America's public schools. The only way we can ever hope to close the achievement gap is by encouraging more heroes like Pedriana to keep pushing against the status quo." —**Jack McCarthy**, managing director, Apple Tree Institute for Education Innovation, Washington, DC

"Pedriana has done an amazing job of covering the data on early reading while at the same time distinguishing between the various research platforms. While there is plenty more to recommend it, on that basis alone *Leaving Johnny Behind* should be required reading for both practicing teachers and those preparing to enter the field." —**Sally Grimes, Ed.M.**, founding director, The Grimes Reading Institute, Rockport, Massachusetts

"I highly recommend this publication for anyone who cares about helping students of all ages learn to read. It is an excellent review of the unfortunate swing of the pendulum over the years about the importance of using phonics to teach reading." —**Joan Sedita**, founding partner, *Keys to Literacy*

"With *Leaving Johnny Behind*, Pedriana takes an important step as an educator, putting his finger on both what we need and where we've failed. He makes it easier for other educators to do the same, so we can all move forward and fix what's broken." —**Steven P. Dykstra, Ph.D.,** Wisconsin Reading Coalition

"As a parent who raised a child who struggled to learn to read, Pedriana's book provides valuable insight for understanding the needs of struggling readers. This book is thus a gift to administrators, educators, parents, and students who want to improve the system but often don't have the background knowledge and voice to advocate for those most in need of educational advocacy. *Leaving Johnny Behind* provides hope that improvement will take place." —**Norma Garza**, member, National Reading Panel

"Pedriana has captured the essence of what is wrong in public school education; teachers are not given the education, tools, mentors, professional development, and support required to teach our children to read. Education and the systems that support it are broken. This book eloquently outlines the scientific studies of how children learn to read. Reading mastery for ALL of our students can happen, but only if we have the courage to acknowledge our mistakes and change the systems that have hurt so many." —**Cheryl Ward**, president, Wisconsin Branch of the International Dyslexia Association

"For the past twenty-five years, I have worked around the country with students who have struggled in learning to read and with teachers who have tried to help them. In *Leaving Johnny Behind*, Pedriana exposes the educational community's unwillingness to embrace best practices identified through legitimate science and the tragic consequences of that failure on both children and their teachers." —**John Alexander**, head of school, Groves Academy, St. Louis Park, Minnesota

"Pedriana has carefully researched the data and eloquently written about what we must do to meet the needs of struggling readers. He clearly shows that there is no longer a reason to leave Johnny—or Julianna—or any other at-risk reader behind." —**Wendy Gaal**, parent, reading teacher, and literacy advocate

Leaving Johnny Behind

Overcoming Barriers to Literacy and Reclaiming At-Risk Readers

Second Edition

Anthony Pedriana

Foreword by G. Reid Lyon

ROWMAN & LITTLEFIELD EDUCATION
A division of
ROWMAN & LITTLEFIELD PUBLISHERS, INC.
Lanham • New York • Toronto • Plymouth, UK

Published by Rowman & Littlefield Education
A division of Rowman & Littlefield Publishers, Inc.
A wholly owned subsidiary of The Rowman & Littlefield Publishing Group, Inc.
4501 Forbes Boulevard, Suite 200, Lanham, Maryland 20706
http://www.rowmaneducation.com

Estover Road, Plymouth PL6 7PY, United Kingdom

British Library Cataloguing in Publication Information Available

Library of Congress Cataloging-in-Publication Data

Pedriana, Anthony.
  Leaving Johnny behind : overcoming barrier to literacy and reclaiming at-risk
readers / Anthony Pedriana. — Second ed.
     p. cm.
  Includes bibliographical references and index.
  ISBN 978-1-60709-912-3 (cloth : alk. paper) — ISBN 978-1-60709-913-0 (pbk. :
alk. paper) — ISBN 978-1-60709-914-7 (electronic)
  1. Reading (Early childhood) 2. Reading—Remedial teaching. 3. Children with
disabilities—Education. I. Title.
  LB1139.5.R43P43 2010
  372.43—dc22   2010019031

∞™ The paper used in this publication meets the minimum requirements of
American National Standard for Information Sciences—Permanence of Paper
for Printed Library Materials, ANSI/NISO Z39.48-1992.

Printed in the United States of America

To my wife, Mary Jo,
without whose unending support
this book could not have been written.
I dedicate it to her, our children,
Gina and Scott, Nick and Teri,
and to our grandchildren,
Rosa and Sophia.

Contents

Foreword

Leaving Johnny Behind: Overcoming Barriers to Literacy and Reclaiming At-Risk Readers is a gift to anyone who desires to understand why so many of our most vulnerable citizens—our children—struggle to learn to read and why we, as a country, have let them down.

With this book, Anthony Pedriana has given to the nation, and particularly the education community, a comprehensive examination of the barriers that prevent kids from becoming proficient readers. Many might be surprised to learn that some of the greatest barriers are constructed by the adults who are responsible for teaching them to read. He provides a clear road map for moving beyond the persistent ideological debates—better known as "the reading wars"—that have plagued the field of reading and have actually prevented many youngsters from learning to read proficiently. While he lays out the reasons for the great divide between reading educators over how to teach reading, he does not engage in the type of emotional diatribe used by many to argue their points of view and the righteousness of their positions.

The contributions this book brings to the field of education are due, in part, to his focus on bringing reading educators together on those instructional principles that all agree are essential to literacy for all. Pedriana brings a tremendous amount of credibility to his task. He is a thirty-five-year veteran of the schools. Throughout that time, he kept reading-level ability for all children at the top of his agenda. Like me, he came to discover, through his teaching, that some of the instructional practices he was using were simply not effective with many struggling readers.

These practices were based on the noble idea that students could learn to read "naturally" by being exposed to rich literature and opportunities to engage in free-flowing literacy interactions. Within this context, emerging readers became proficient by constructing their own knowledge about our reading system and did not require a systematic, "teacher-centered" approach to help them navigate the linguistic complexities of our English language. As Pedriana points out, many educators eschewed systematic and explicit instruction because of the belief that "drill and kill" methods would stifle a child's love for reading. He also explains that it is hard to love something that you cannot do—a commonsense realization that many educators have still not achieved.

Like me, after seeing the frustration and fear in the eyes of many students when asked to read, Pedriana came to the conclusion that there had to be a better way to teach students to become proficient readers. And, like me, he takes responsibility for letting many kids down and he feels some guilt about that.

This book is a reflection of Pedriana's journey into the world of evidence-based reading instruction, including the conditions under which this instruction is most effective, and for which kids. You will note, however, that the new insights he gained are not used to bludgeon educators with different perspectives. Rather, he explains—in very thoughtful prose—that there are situations where multiple perspectives will serve the child.

What you will find as you read this book is that Pedriana is a true champion for kids who are struggling to learn the most important set of skills that will enable them to flourish in school and in life. He makes it clear that our children are our nation's most important and cherished gift. They represent the legacy of our efforts to provide a safe and nurturing world for them. They also embody our hopes and dreams for the future.

Yet it became abundantly clear to him that, in addition to the struggling readers in his classrooms, millions of other children also entered pre-school and kindergarten without the language and literacy skills needed to succeed in school and in life. And, with this book, Pedriana teaches us how we can improve this state of affairs.

No doubt I am biased in my appreciation for his compelling and riveting story. I have spent over thirty years trying to answer three simple questions:

1. How do children learn to read?
2. Why do so many kids have difficulties learning to read?
3. How can we best help them become proficient readers?

My involvement in the research to address these three questions began in 1978 and took place at Northwestern University, the University of Vermont, and, finally, the National Institutes of Health. The research was conducted by over four hundred developmental scientists from multiple disciplines studying well over forty thousand children at forty-four sites nationally and internationally. It took over twenty years to even come close to answering the questions. And the answers that were found came to serve as the scientific building blocks for what is now termed "scientifically based reading instruction."

But much of what we found simply validated Pedriana's observations over his career as a teacher, principal, and mentor to principals. For example, we found that the majority of the youngsters who have reading difficulties have something in common; they are poor. And, as Pedriana points out, they are victims of discrimination. Yet, despite over forty years of expensive federal programs to bolster prereading and language abilities of poor children during the preschool years and every instructional fad you can imagine that descended on our public schools, the literacy gap between children of advantage and children of disadvantage has not changed.

Does it have to be this way? NO! We have ample evidence that early identification and evidence-based prevention programs can virtually wipe out this gap, if implemented appropriately.

Unfortunately, we found that the gap widens and accelerates with each grade. Eighty-eight percent of youngsters who read poorly at the end of the first grade read poorly at the end of the fourth grade. Students who have not caught up by nine years of age carry their limited reading skills into adulthood. Those students who have not learned to read by the ninth grade typically drop out of school at significantly higher rates than their classmates who read proficiently.

Reading failure is invasive and cumulative. Without proficient reading skills, many of these kids are doomed to lifelong hardship with little potential for occupational, economic, and social advancement. They are more likely to become teen parents, end up in prison, and suffer from persistent health problems. Without aggressive and innovative approaches to prevent reading failure, a bleak future awaits many of these children. This is an American tragedy.

As Pedriana points out, this is why effective, scientifically based instruction is so darned important. Unlike their more advantaged agemates, many kids from low-income homes have never been read to while sitting on their parents' laps and have not heard stories read at bedtime. It could be that their parents do not read themselves. It could be that paying for food has a higher priority than paying for books. Whatever the reason, low income typically means a limited number of (or no) books in the home, not to mention the absence of magnetic letters, drawing paper, newspapers, and other reading-related materials. It is very difficult for children to develop emergent literacy skills when they do not have access to these resources. We have no choice—it is up to the teachers to pick up the slack.

Poor children hear fewer words at home and have limited conversations with adults. Many have learned only half the words they must know when they enter kindergarten, and, more often than not, they will not know the letters of the alphabet or how to follow words from left to right across the printed page. By the ninth grade, many have the vocabulary of a third-grade student. Without these essential early reading and language abilities, most will carry the baggage of illiteracy into their adult years, increasing the chances that their own kids won't learn to read either. Again, we have no choice—teachers have to pick up the slack.

Leaving Johnny Behind: Overcoming Barriers to Literacy and Reclaiming At-Risk Readers lets us know clearly that it does not have to be this way. While we may not be able to address all the problems caused by poverty, the good news is that we can overcome illiteracy. Research at the National Institutes of Health and elsewhere indicates that the number of children who suffer from reading failure, and thus failure in school, can be reduced significantly *if* they begin kindergarten and first grade with the essential language and reading-readiness abilities, followed by effective reading instruction after school entry. The National Research Council estimated that, if children receive proper exposure and systematic opportunities to develop foundational language, reading, and emergent writing skills during early childhood, as few as 5 percent may experience serious reading difficulty. Likewise, our research found that evidence-based interventions with older struggling readers in inner-city schools could reduce reading difficulties to less than 10 percent.

Pedriana has summarized much of this research in very clear language and brings it to life by showing how scientific findings can inform both policy and instructional practices. He also asks a question that many of us have posed ad nauseum: Why is it that many educators simply won't use research evidence to guide their practices? To put a finer point on it, if research is so critical to continually improving practice in other fields relevant to the health and welfare of children, then why do some of those on the front lines of education, such as teachers and administrators, frequently view research in education as trivial or irrelevant? And even when a scientific breakthrough has occurred (e.g., the discovery that phonemic awareness is essential to reading development), what is it about the field of education that makes translating, disseminating, and implementing the findings so difficult?

We now have some answers to these questions and I think these answers are essential if we are to overcome the barriers to implementing research findings. One reason (that should come as no surprise to anyone in the field of education) is that a decidedly anti-scientific spirit has had a pervasive influence on the perceived value of research. The most current cycle of education's reluctance to use scientific evidence stems, as Pedriana points out, from the philosophy of postmodernism, which, in its most dramatic form, states that truth is relative, in the eye of the beholder, and framed only by one's own experience and culture.

The most hard-line version of postmodernism claims that general cause-effect principles do not exist in the world. Thus, scientific methods that seek to identify them are not useful for education decision making and practice. Indeed, over the past two decades, data that could dispel some wacky assertions about student learning and achievement that arose from philosophical, ideological, and political beliefs were often not accumulated or disseminated. As a result, untested claims have often trumped scientific facts. It is fascinating that a substantial number of educators and non-educators who see the value of scientific research in fields such as health care and industry fail to see the contributions it can make to education.

To be sure, university faculty and researchers should take a lot of responsibility for the attitudes many educators have about "research" and their teaching. Many schools of education do not typically prepare future teachers to value the use of research to inform their instructional practices or provide them with the knowledge and skills to keep abreast of the scientific literature in their field. Debra Viadero, reporting for *Education Week* in 2003, wrote, "Even if teachers have the fortitude to plow through academic journals, chances are their professional training did not include coursework in how to distinguish good research from bad."

So, we find ourselves in this situation: less than one-third of the instructional practices used by teachers are based on scientific research findings. Even when evidence-based practices are used, teachers cannot clearly explain why they have used them. When asked, many teachers report that educational research is trivial and irrelevant to their teaching, is too theoretical and complex, and communicated in an incomprehensible manner. School principals and school administrators trained at the doctoral level are equally reluctant to use research to guide their leadership efforts and infuse research-based practices in their districts and schools.

Recently, Arthur Levine, past president of Teacher's College at Columbia University, reported that only 56 percent of principals, for example, found that the research courses they took in their degree programs were valuable to their jobs. A major reason cited was that the courses were too abstract—emphasizing mechanistic aspects of research designs and methods without clear examples of how research can be applied to inform practice in schools and classrooms. In short, the courses emphasized form over function without integrating the two. On the line in the classrooms, many teachers find themselves attempting to implement the latest highly touted instructional "magic bullet" only to learn, after it fails, that the research upon which it was based was seriously flawed.

Even more frustrating for educational consumers is that the majority of such programs, methods, and educational products today claim to be "research-based" despite having little or no scientifically sound evidence of effectiveness. Until educational practitioners are properly trained to ensure that they can discriminate between rigorous and valid research and research that was poorly designed, frustration will increase and the market for even the best research will continue to decrease.

What is so unique about this book is that Pedriana has addressed all these thorny issues, shown how they keep us from teaching kids to read, and then posed several questions asked from the perspective of a veteran educator. He is clearly a scientist-practitioner. He has taken us on a fascinating journey in this book that blazes new territory in our understanding of why Johnny has been left behind—and, more importantly, what we can do about it. He has provided us with a superb continuation to the field and to the education of our most cherished gift—our kids.

—Reid Lyon, Ph.D., Distinguished Professor of Education Policy and Leadership, Southern Methodist University, Dallas; Distinguished Scientist, School of Brain and Behavior Sciences, University of Texas, Dallas

Message from the Author

Building more and better readers was a matter that confounded me throughout my career. It just didn't seem right that so many of our kids failed to meet proficiency requirements, and I always suspected there had to be a better way to meet their needs. Finding those ways was supposed to be the purview of academicians whose job it was to conduct empirical investigations and pass along their findings to those of us in the so-called trenches. I saw it as being akin to how medical research guided medical practice. But it doesn't seem to work that way in education, and, specifically, it doesn't appear that reading science has much influence on how reading is generally taught.

None of this is meant to absolve me of anything. I always had strong opinions about what worked best for kids and I could be as sanctimonious and intractable in defense of those opinions as anyone. If there was indeed a better way and I could not find it in all my thirty-five years in the field, then that said as much about me as anyone else, and I must be as accountable as the next person. And, if I find that my efforts were at times misguided and ill-advised, that certainly will not make my twilight years any easier.

All I know is, even from the comfort of my retirement perch, the matter continues to haunt me, but I refuse to go to my grave rationalizing that I worked hard and did my best. It wasn't about working hard and doing my best—it was about making kids read. I recall the superintendent telling us at one of our monthly meetings, "It's good that you all work hard. But you must also work smart. If you do that, you may not need to work quite so hard." That caused a few nervous twitters among some, myself included. I knew that I worked hard, but that did not distinguish me in any way. We all worked hard. Whether I worked smart was another matter.

And so, while I wrote this narrative from the perspective of one with a vision concerning children's literacy attainment, I also wrote it as a way to confront the reality of my own performance, a chance, perhaps, to exorcise my demons, so to speak. You can thus call it what you want—a retrospective, a reflection, a personal assessment—whatever you choose. But the fact of the matter is, my advanced age has not served to diminish my ego or make it any less vulnerable.

So I decided that, if I failed to provide all that was available during my working years, perhaps I could extract some measure of atonement by taking some time to fill in the gaps and relate what I learned to others with a similar mission. In that regard, this is a search for truth, with the most amazing truth being the fact that I somehow had to search for it. I am at once outraged to have learned that those whose role it was to call it to my attention failed to do so and embarrassed to have to admit that I was not smart enough to find it on my own. It's like an experienced physician asking, "You mean you can immunize a kid by actually *giving him the disease*?"

My first impulse was to make this book all about the "reading wars." My narrative would be a continuation of that battle, with me riding in like the cavalry to rescue every kid from a lifetime of illiteracy. But, after a time, I began to realize just how misguided such an approach would be. Most wars are caused by raw emotionalism in righteously indignant people prepared to defend their versions of truth and impose them on others, no matter what the cost. It is easy to see the ramifications of that mind-set in the literal world when innocent people die and countless others are mutilated because adults are incapable of resolving their differences in the same way they expect children to mediate their playground scraps.

Fortunately, the exhortations of a professor of sociology (who happens to be my son) led me to conclude that highlighting the conflict surrounding the reading debates would constitute a failure of mission. Despite my initial anger, I knew, in the end, he was right in asserting that pursuing the war analogy would merely add to a process that has already left far too many children as collateral damage. If I were truly looking to advance the cause of children's literacy, then I would be well-advised to find areas upon which all could agree as opposed to ripping the scabs off old wounds.

This book is, therefore, my attempt to discover and promote a message around which reading practitioners can unite and, in so doing, serve children better than we have in the past. I know my effort may amount to little more than a quixotic lunging at windmills. Please indulge my trying to salvage a bit more from my thirty-five years in the schools and, perhaps, offer something more than what I always did so as to effect something more than what I always got. It may well fall on deaf ears, but at least I will have tried. Right now, that's all I can hope to achieve.

Preface to the Second Edition

Welcome to this, the second edition of *Leaving Johnny Behind*. The main body of text contains a few minor edits but is essentially the same mainly because the message remains constant. In a nutshell, the message is that we have the knowledge and ability to teach all children to read at proficient levels but doing so requires that teachers teach directly, assess frequently, and apply the appropriate interventions immediately. Proceeding in this fashion will allow us to replace the current "wait to fail" model with one in which "failure is not an option."

I would like to use this opportunity, however, to call attention to a couple of changes that involve the cover design and an addition to the Resources for Teachers and Parents section. Following that I will ruminate briefly on the challenges that remain and initiatives that bring renewed hope that we have indeed made inroads on the literacy front since the initial release of *Leaving Johnny Behind* in August of 2009.

COVER DESIGN

Those familiar with the original publication will note the change in cover design, the empty desk having been replaced by an image of a student whose school adjustment appears to be something less than optimal. It was chosen because it captures the isolation, fear, anger, and resentment children experience when they fail to master essential literacy ability on an age-appropriate timeline. My hope is that this depiction of anguish and pain will elicit greater compassion for those who suffer needlessly

and will lend greater urgency to our attempts at meaningful and legitimate reform.

CATALOG OF RESEARCH-BASED READING PROGRAMS

Another change is the inclusion of a list of research-based reading programs, which appears on pages 151–56. I do this reluctantly since there
are those who might surmise that I somehow would stand to profit from
such an enterprise. I can assure the reader that I derive no remuneration
of any kind from any of the publishers nor their subsidiaries. My only
rationale is that I believe strongly that schools and districts should be able
to choose from among programs whose efficacy has been validated by
empirical evidence and clinical application. Perhaps it is best characterized as an expression of consumer activism.

CHALLENGES

While we are beginning to see some movement, formidable obstacles still
remain in the path of legitimate reform. Teacher quality continues to be a
problem mainly because schools of education and state licensing authorities have yet to adequately improve teacher training. In a follow-up to its
2006 landmark study, the National Council on Teacher Quality reported
in 2009 that "Taken as a whole, state teacher policies are broken, outdated
and inflexible."[1]

Specific to the issue of reading, the NCTQ states in Point 5 of the Executive Summary:

> Only 25 states require teacher preparation programs to fully address the sci-
> ence of reading either through coursework requirements or standards that
> programs must meet. Even fewer states make sure that prospective teachers
> actually have acquired this knowledge. Only five states use an appropriate
> rigorous test that ensures teachers are well prepared to teach their students
> to read.[2]

I personally can attest to this intransigence on the part of the educational establishment. When we meet with representatives from higher
education and their partner agencies, they tend to sit, listen, smile be-
nignly, and wait for our contingency to leave. Even the loss of education
dollars meted out through President Barack Obama's Race to the Top
school funding initiative doesn't appear to motivate them to change their
attitude or alter their practices.

Teacher unions also seem reticent to cooperate in such ventures. When calling attention to his state's dismal reading performance on the National Assessment of Educational Progress (NAEP), one union lobbyist contended that the NAEP standards were too high and that NAEP's "basic" category was best interpreted as "proficient." These and other experiences have made it increasingly clear to me that turf battles, political expediency, power, and money continue to wield enormous negative influence on the literacy futures of countless children.

ENCOURAGING SIGNS

As bleak as all of that sounds, there are also countless signs of encouragement. On the federal level, we are seeing bipartisan efforts to address the reading crisis. President Obama is building on initiatives largely set forth by his republican predecessor George W. Bush whose No Child Left Behind Act was based on findings revealed through the Reading Excellence Act under Bill Clinton. While No Child Left Behind will be reauthorized, tweaked, and renamed, we have seen that the government is remaining steadfast in its attempts to stop squandering good money on questionable practices. I think most would see that as a good thing regardless of whether they are liberal or conservative, republican or democrat.

The LEARN Act

Also in the works is the LEARN Act (Literacy Education for All Results for the Nation) which authorizes the Secretary of Education to award grants to states for comprehensive planning to improve the literacy of children from birth through grade 12. Both the house and senate versions seek to: "Provide strategic, systematic, and explicit instruction in phonological awareness, phonic decoding, vocabulary, reading fluency, and reading comprehension."[3] This kind of specificity helps cut off escape routes of those ideologues who have been remarkably successful at evading such governmental edicts in the past.

Union Cooperation

We may also be seeing the dawn of a new spirit of cooperation between school districts and teacher unions. At the time of this writing Randi Weingarten, president of the American Federation of Teachers, and Michelle Rhee, chancellor of the Washington, D.C., schools had reached a tentative agreement on a new contract to address education reform. Such reform would seek to remove restrictions that prohibit districts from basing teacher evaluation on student performance and to revise tenure rules that all too often provide a safe harbor for marginal educators.

Administrative Leadership

New ground is also being broken in our quest to build a more effective corps of school administrators. Under the leadership of Reid Lyon, the Annette Caldwell School of Education at Southern Methodist University is developing a graduate program in administrative leadership that will assure that its clients receive training grounded in the most unassailable expressions of scientific inquiry, an attribute that is sorely lacking in most traditional venues. What makes the program at SMU even more significant, however, is that it is seeking to make itself as accountable for student advancement as those it puts on the front lines. In its Narrative on Vision, Lyon writes:

> The mission of the SMU programs in Education Policy and Leadership is focused on, and defined by, the impact our graduates ultimately have on the learning and achievement of the students in their districts and schools.[4]

If all schools of education were to accept this measure of accountability, those about to enter the field would have an exponentially greater chance of succeeding where their predecessors had failed. Hopefully, other institutions for higher learning will begin to replicate this model, a phenomenon that would surely be a cause for celebration for all of us.

Moms on a Mission

I expected to receive some support for the message I had put forth in *Leaving Johnny Behind* but felt that mine would essentially be a voice in the wilderness. The exact opposite has turned out to be the case, and perhaps that is what I find most encouraging of all. The truth is that many organizations have launched a frontal assault on our literacy crisis using the fundamental truth of investigative science as their most powerful weapon. These organizations are disproportionately comprised of women, and I have lost count of the number who tell virtually identical stories.

1. Their child experiences reading difficulty.
2. They seek help from the school and get nowhere.
3. They investigate matters on their own and discover the disconnect between what their child needs and what he or she gets.

4. They either find a school that offers the appropriate services or they do it on their own.

They may struggle, and they may waver, but rarely do they fail nor do they quit even after they have secured their own child's literacy future. Instead, they find one another, mobilize, and continue to press forward on behalf of others with similar experiences.

Their expressions of commitment are legion, Moms on a Mission as one group dubs itself. They do their own research, provide workshops, mobilize in support of literacy legislation, and work vigorously to make the fruit of their efforts available to all who have need for it. In so doing, they endure all manner of hardship and resistance and are willing to take on negative characterizations among the reading establishment if that is what it takes to extract some measure of compliance. They do all of this on their own time and at their own expense. I draw strength and energy merely by being in their company. If anyone is to be perceived as leaders and heroes, it is surely they, and I am indeed fortunate to have crossed paths with so many of them.

NOTES

1. *2009 State Teacher Policy Yearbook: National Summary,* National Council on Teacher Quality, 5.

2. *2009 State Teacher Policy Yearbook,* 7.

3. U.S. Senate Bill 2740-Section 4, (1), (B), (iii). Similar language is found in the House of Representatives Bill 4037-Section 13, (7), (B), (i).

4. Reid Lyon, "Leadership: Courage and Possibility—Filling the Leadership Void in Education," Programs in Educational Policy and Leadership at Southern Methodist University, 12.

Prologue

Simulated Courtroom Drama, Circa 2000

Prosecutor: *What, sir, is your name and occupation?*

Defendant: *My name is Anthony Pedriana, and I am an elementary school principal.*

Prosecutor: *Mr. Pedriana, was it not your responsibility to assure that the students in your school received appropriate reading instruction?*

Defendant: *Yes, sir, it certainly was.*

Prosecutor: *In that regard—that is, in teaching children to read—is it not true that you chose to use some rather unconventional strategies?*

Defendant: *Yes, I suppose some might have considered them unconventional.*

Prosecutor: *And what were these so-called unconventional methods?*

Defendant: *Well, we used something called the alphabetic principle. You know, the kind of thing where kids are taught the relationship between letters and sounds.*

Prosecutor: *I see. And at what age would you begin teaching children this alphabetic stuff?*

Defendant: *As soon as possible. Five-years-old—earlier if we thought they were ready.*

Prosecutor: *Would you characterize the manner in which you taught alphabetics as being somewhat unconventional also?*

1

Defendant:	*Well, perhaps. Our methods were very directed and system-atized. Some might consider that unusual.*
Prosecutor:	*By directed and systematized, don't you mean drill-based?*
Defendant:	*Yes, it did involve some drill. We practiced until we were sure the students had mastered each skill.*
Prosecutor:	*Are you aware, sir, that many in your profession characterize such practices as developmentally inappropriate for children that age?*
Defendant:	*I've heard that school of thought, yes.*
Prosecutor:	*And despite the generally accepted view in your profession that such tactics were developmentally inappropriate, did you never-theless continue to use these same procedures?*
Defendant:	*Yes, I continued to apply these practices in my school until I retired.*
Prosecutor:	*Do I hear you right, sir, when you admit in front of this court, that you subjected children at the young and impressionable age of five-years-old to endless and mindless drill-based tactics?*
Defendant:	*Well, no, I wouldn't call them endless and mindless. In fact . . .*
Prosecutor:	*Your Honor, the prosecution rests.*

Many may view the preceding as a contemptuous way to portray the angst that has characterized early reading instruction for so long. However, I am comfortable in asserting that this attempt at pseudodrama reflects the defensive position in which I found myself when I implemented a reading program that applied direct and systematic instruction in the alphabetic principle to children at the earliest of levels.

I realize that, by merely pointing this out, I run the risk of losing my audience, those of you who lay your collective souls on the line each and every day on behalf of children, as well as others aspiring to do the same. I run that risk because it is hard to talk about *anything* related to reading pedagogy without alienating one faction or another. The battles have been characterized in different ways but they have changed little over the years. It's back-to-basics versus progressivism, phonics versus whole-language, code-based versus meaning-based, liberal versus conservative, research-based versus non-research-based, and on and on.

So, as precarious as it is to roil those waters once again, I nevertheless must try. I must try because what I have found is that the whole debate is essentially a fraud. And the notion that we must draw lines in the sand over these issues while children fail to master essential literacy skills is a betrayal of our high-minded expressions of *children first*.

And so I implore you, the reader, not to abandon this narrative in its early stages, but to at least listen to the positions I have taken on these crucial matters and join me on the path that led me to discover them:

1. I am in favor of practices that have withstood the introspective lens of scientific inquiry. (*Now wait . . . hold on . . . keep reading.*)
2. Therefore, I am in favor of alphabetic training at early levels. (*I know this one isn't helping. But hold on for 3 and 4. It will get better, I promise.*)
3. I am in favor of alphabetic training at early levels only when such instruction enhances a child's ability to construct meaning from print. (*Okay, just one more.*)
4. Therefore, I am not opposed to the various forms of constructivism, such as whole-language, because there can be no doubt that deriving meaning from print is central to their purpose as well.

Even those of you who have continued to read are likely to view those statements with skepticism, interpreting them as nothing more than straddling the fence and trying to have it both ways. You would be right. You would be right because mounds of empirical evidence state in unequivocal terms that *not only can we have it both ways, but we should have it both ways.* What the data say, over and over again, is that mastery of the alphabetic code and the ability to construct meaning from an integrated whole are companion skills. When properly applied, they advance one another's cause and, thereby, form a symbiotic relationship that lends dynamism and power to our efforts. Embracing one of those to the degree that it leads to the exclusion of the other represents a wholesale abandonment of Johnny and all his cohorts.

This is the unifying message that has resonated from the science of reading over the past four decades. However, despite the fact that science essentially builds a bridge between what have been competing pedagogies, some would have us believe otherwise. They would view my decision to incorporate direct and systematic code-based practices into our daily reading activities as an abandonment of principle. They would see it as a schismatic departure from acceptable practice, one that was sure to compromise children's motivation, rob them of their self-esteem, and replace the joy and wonder of learning to read with a daily regimen of dull and dispiriting drills.

My attempt to carry on in such an environment uncovered just how dissonant and fragmented were the guidelines used to foster reading-skills development and the inadvertent and counterintuitive role this disharmony played in keeping children from attaining essential literacy skills. I found the matter so disheartening that I have spent a good share of my retirement trying to determine what could have led to such a sad state of affairs and why those bent on serving children have found so little unanimity on their behalf. The following narrative thus describes my personal journey to attempt to resolve that dichotomy.

SEPARATE AND UNEQUAL

I learned early on that poor teaching and/or flawed methodologies can compromise nearly any child's advancement toward literacy, but that most are in a position to overcome such obstacles. Others, however, are far less fortunate. As is the case in so many other domains, it is the poor and disenfranchised who suffer disproportionately from adult failures. And one of the primary causes of this failure stems from the fact that few have the courage to state the obvious for fear of being seen as insensitive, misguided, and naïve. Regardless of how I might be perceived for saying so, poor kids are more likely to suffer trauma from the time they are conceived and throughout their lives. They have less access to resources and are less likely to inherit the kind of family stability that will enhance their chances for success.

I realize this is a societal problem, the solution to which has evaded humankind throughout its existence. But to invoke that stance is perhaps to suggest that some children are just destined to be left behind. I don't believe that and I would venture to guess that anyone who has read to this point doesn't believe it either. We all realize it is our job to confront such inequities and do our best to mitigate them. My investigation of how we might best do that has led me to discover that, when it comes to literacy training, there are some truths out there that we have failed to recognize and others we have adamantly refused to consider even when they were brought to our attention. This book is, therefore, written on behalf of the victims of those failures, those who, through no faults of their own, find themselves at risk of failing to achieve the most fundamental and essential tool for life success.

The following are brief summaries of the chapters to follow:

Chapter 1: A Failure to Communicate. Sets out some introductory evidence that research-based techniques for teaching reading are not being used and speculates on the causes of this condition.

Chapter 2: Gayle Force. Describes an experience late in my career that caused me to discover an alternative approach to reading instruction and to modify my beliefs about early reading methodology.

Chapter 3: Soporific Effluvium. Provides some historical background in order to better understand the conflicts that have kept the matter of early reading in a constant state of disequilibrium and, perhaps, explain their influence on the current state of affairs.

Chapter 4: Preponderance of the Evidence. Reviews the findings of nine major research syntheses on the subject of early reading.

Chapter 5: Uniformity Unhinged. Describes the educational community's response to the data, and draws some distinctions between research platforms.

Chapter 6: The Weak Arm of the Law. Describes events that led to Congress's enactment of the No Child Left Behind legislation and its impact on educational practice throughout the country.

Chapter 7: So Shall We Reap. Examines the impact of reading failure on individuals and society.

Chapter 8: The Unkindest Cut of All. Describes the untenable position we assign to teachers when we deny them training based on reading science.

Chapter 9: The 3 Rs—Reform, Reform, Reform. Takes a critical look at the impact of school-reform measures.

Chapter 10: Teaching to Mastery. Depicts the kind of direct and systematic reading instruction that adheres strictly to the recommendations of the data.

Chapter 11: Through Johnny's Eyes. Chronicles the life of a student left behind in the quest for literacy attainment.

Chapter 12: Rescuing Johnny. A challenge to the educational community to bring about true reform through strict adherence to the scientific message.

1

⤝⤞

A Failure to Communicate

"We have met the enemy, and he is us."

—Walt Kelly, Pogo

Early literacy is among the most powerful predictors of school success, gainful employment, and societal adjustment. For that reason, I long ago determined that the sincerest and most powerful expression of child advocacy was insisting on reading-level proficiency for all. Reading ability gives to youngsters an eternal source of joy, hope, and esteem and represents the single most essential tool that will allow them to lead well-adjusted and productive lives. And, because it is so vital, those of us in the schools need to know how best to go about accomplishing it. For that, I had always followed in the truest of liberal traditions.

Acceptable practices were those that operated from what came to be known as a constructivist dynamic, one that called for individuals to construct meaning based on their prior knowledge and experience instead of regurgitating some kind of prepackaged skill base or someone else's version of the right answers. In that regard, curriculum was to be child-centered, respecting each youngster's individual path to literacy. Repetitive measures of any kind were antithetical to this approach, developmentally inappropriate at early levels, and, therefore, to be avoided at all cost.

I didn't just stumble onto these notions. These were the ideals that undergirded all my training as an undergraduate and graduate student and throughout most of my career as a teacher and administrator. It was hard to argue against the idea that such practices had served the needs of the majority.

Still I knew that too many had gotten past us, had failed to advance to appropriate levels. We tried to do better by those kids, modifying our strategies, providing individual and small-group instruction, integrating curriculum, building background knowledge, expending untold amounts of energy to address specific needs. We were encouraged to innovate and/or do whatever we felt could work, as long as we continued to operate within the parameters of "child-centrism."

The freedom this afforded allowed us to trust in ourselves. We always had hope for those who struggled, we always exuded optimism that we could meet their needs, and we always had faith in the principles that reflected our training. What we didn't have was any measure of specificity, any assurance that if we employed a particular strategy and practiced it faithfully day in and day out, then achievement would be the natural by-product of our work. Perhaps there is no such magical formula, but, even if none existed, I was sure we could do better than we had in the past. You will have to excuse me if I choose to take the oft-heard mantra, "All children can learn," in a literal sense and not merely as a matter of political correctness.

A NEW LOOK AT AN OLD PARADIGM

We've all heard the old adage telling us that, "If you always do what you always did, you will always get what you always got." We were not getting nearly enough, and children were paying the price. It was time to look at the situation from a radically different perspective. We certainly wanted to provide instruction that was child-centered, but what was child-centric about a condition where often one-third to one-half of a class was reading below level? Perhaps my conception of child-centrism was seriously flawed or omitted some important elements.

This bit of soul-searching began when I learned that empirical evidence had shown support for a reading method that ran contrary to the conventional wisdom. The approach was based on the premise that early literacy instruction required direct, intensive, and systematic use of the alphabetic principle—a measure that contradicted nearly all we had been taught. How, I wondered, could there be such a contradiction between what science recommended and what normally occurred in classrooms?

A FAILURE TO COMMUNICATE

It wasn't until my career had ended that I had the opportunity to investigate this disconnect and its effects on children's literacy. The results of that personal journey are now between the covers of this book, and it has indeed been a fascinating one.

First, I got a glimpse into the academic turf battles that have played themselves out in this country for nearly one hundred and fifty years. I found the debates often went beyond the parameters of polite discourse and, all too often, were more about adults than kids.

Second, I discovered that I was largely oblivious to a knowledge base that spoke to the matter of early reading in clear, resonant, and definitive terms. It was a unifying message that combined the meaning-based dynamic of constructivism and the phonics-based model that stressed the relationship between sound and symbol. Normally these two constructs were viewed as oppositional forces, but my analysis of the research revealed that they were companion skills that enhanced rather than undermined one another.

It was perplexing to think that educators could not find a way to coalesce around such a unifying message and use it to drive education policy at the national, state, and district levels. But that has indeed been the case because a wide gap continues to exist between what the research recommends and the practices that dominate early reading instruction. How could we claim to put children first when the matter of early literacy training was relegated to little more than a shot in the dark, a virtual crapshoot on behalf of those who needed us the most? As the jailer so eloquently put it to Paul Newman's title character in *Cool Hand Luke*, "What we have here is a failure to communicate."

FINDING TRUE NORTH

What is the cause of this communications breakdown? My foray into the reading debates caused me to conclude that, if we must look to blame anyone, it should be those who operate from extremist positions and who choose to remain intractable in the face of overwhelming evidence. Their writings are often so emotion-driven that they come off as diatribes, expressions of an ideology that will not tolerate one iota of dissent. And, yet, they continue to wield enormous power and influence over the manner in which reading is taught throughout the English-speaking world.

How can we avoid such pitfalls? How do we focus with laser-like intensity on the goal of reaching kids we have failed for so long? It baffled me as to why we would choose to act contrary to the manner in which humankind has always addressed its most significant challenges—by giving children the benefit of instruction revealed through rigorous science. The raw power of scientific inquiry has always been the ultimate revealer of truth. It has no political agendas, no faith-based assumptions, and no

cultural sensibilities. Its ability to ignore all such extraneous and dissonant factors has allowed us to eradicate disease, design buildings that can
withstand earthquakes, and isolate the fastest and best ways to regenerate
forests. In my mind, to base reading practice on anything else is to mock
the very notion of child-centrism.

Remarkably, however, there are some who have chosen to demonize
the science that has, and continues to, run counter to what they would
recommend. I will attempt to clarify issues related to the science of reading in succeeding chapters, but, for now, it is important to make the
reader aware of how successful a few have been at keeping the research
message out of classrooms and, thus, causing us to betray our promise to
filter our every decision based on what works best for kids. To make that
point, I refer to a report to Congress by Duane Alexander, then the director of the National Institute of Child Health and Human Development.[1]

Alexander noted the scientific progress sponsored by his agency in
dealing with three critical public health issues for children: sudden infant
death syndrome (SIDS), spina bifida, and reading failure. When science
discovered the relationship between SIDS and babies' sleep positions,
the medical community wasted no time in getting the information out to
parents who immediately began altering the manner in which they placed
their infants in their cribs. A second area of progress was the science that
identified the role of folic acid metabolism in causing spina bifida and
other neo- and post-natal birth defects. The response there was to create
legislation requiring that all bread be fortified with Vitamin B.

Not surprisingly, after these actions, investigators noted an immediate
reduction in both SIDS and spina bifida.

But the third area of progress mentioned by Alexander involved the
knowledge gained about reading and reading failure. The story there
was quite different, as evidenced by the testimony to Congress of Benita
Blackman, a well-known reading researcher:

> The good news is that there have been scientific breakthroughs in our knowl-
> edge about the development of literacy. We know a great deal about how
> to address reading problems even before they begin. The tragedy is that we
> are not exploiting what is known about reducing the incidence of reading
> failure. Specifically, the instruction currently being provided to our children
> does not reflect what we know from the research. Direct, systematic instruc-
> tion about the alphabetic code is not routinely being provided in kindergar-
> ten and first grade despite the fact that, given what we know at the moment,
> this might be the most powerful weapon in the fight against illiteracy.[2]

All this would be much easier to understand if literacy rates were on
the rise and we weren't continuing to see ever-widening achievement
gaps that disproportionately affect poor and minority populations. In

light of that, it is hard to refrain from questioning the motives of a few. Is it really about teaching kids to read or might it reflect some other agenda? Maybe there was a career to validate or an ax to grind. Perhaps it was nothing more than professional self-absorption run amok or blind loyalty to a creed that had somehow managed to interfere with one's true purpose—"true north," as Stephen Covey would call it.[3]

Nevertheless, many still continue to engage in ideological cherry picking and, in so doing, demonstrate hypocrisy in its purest form. These tactics keep the true message of science from reaching those on the front lines and result in an ever-changing interfusion of the latest innovations, modifications, and gimmicks. Those who choose to pursue "research-based" practices are condemned for having done so, thus confirming our suspicion that a lot of what happens in classrooms is not based on research. When one ponders the needs of a child who has no choice but to rely on adults to do the right thing, one can only utter in bewilderment, "Say it ain't so."

A CALL FOR UNITY

In any event, I am not so naïve as to think I can change the opinions of those who would attempt to stifle or obfuscate what science has to say about early reading or those who are unwilling even to consider that there truly is a middle ground that can work for all of us. I will not even attempt to do so.

But I can appeal to the vast majority of educators who have never lost sight of their mission. These are dedicated individuals open to anything that will assist them in making readers of each and every child who comes under their tutelage, regardless of the challenge any one of them might pose. And most, I suspect, would be only too happy to avail themselves of an opportunity to get the kind of training that best reflects the research message, if only some experts would dismount from their pedagogical high horses and make it available to them.

There are, however, powerful forces that stand in the way. The very term "research-based" is politically charged because its ubiquitous support for code-based measures causes many to associate it with religious zealotry and/or arch-conservatism, part of a right-wing agenda that challenges progressive thought. I do not wish to engage in that argument. But, let's just assume for a second that it is true, and that some might have ulterior motives for pushing code-based practices. Are we to disregard the scientific message on that basis alone? Are we to assume that political opposites must always be at cross-purposes with one another? Should we ignore decades of empirical evidence simply because those we dislike embrace it so voraciously?

I just have a hard time understanding how that works to any child's advantage. The truth of the matter is, accepting the research message and giving it adequate expression in classrooms need not be perceived as either a validation of conservative values or a subversion of progressive thought. Much to the contrary, it represents an opportunity we seldom experience, one that has the potential to transcend ideology and bring synergy to our efforts to make proficient readers of all our children. Imagine that: conservatives and liberals converging in pursuit of literacy for all. It would be a contradiction in terms if those of us who deem ourselves true progressives squandered such a chance.

NOTES

1. Fletcher and Lyon, "Reading: A Research-Based Approach," in *What's Gone Wrong in America's Classrooms*, 50.
2. Fletcher and Lyon, "Reading: A Research-Based Approach," 50.
3. Covey, Merrill, and Merrill, *First Things First*, 51.

2

⊂✍◎

Gayle Force

"The path of least resistance and least trouble is a mental rut already made. It requires troublesome work to undertake the alternation of old beliefs."

—John Dewey

It began in August of 1997 as I was nearing retirement as an elementary school principal in Milwaukee's central city. At that point, my career had spanned nearly thirty years, two-thirds of which had been spent as a classroom teacher. I had liked to think that, during all that time, I had lived and breathed child advocacy. In fact, heeding the advice of pop psychology, I had taken the time to write my personal mission statement. There it was, scribbled on a piece of paper and inserted at the front of my daily planner: "To serve as an advocate for children and to do any and all things possible to support teachers in their efforts to do the same." If I wrote it down, it must be true, right? And what better way to advocate for children than to do all in my power to make proficient readers of each and every one of them?

But it was one thing to write it down and another to make it happen. And it wasn't happening, at least not to an acceptable degree. In any given year, 30 percent or more of our kids exited their grade reading below level and leaving us to scratch our heads and wonder what else we might have done. Was that to be my legacy? "He did a good job; he just failed to meet the needs of a third of his clients." Would you send your kid to a doctor with a record like that?

It wasn't for lack of trying. We had a dedicated staff that worked tire-lessly and endlessly on behalf of their pupils. Together, we marshaled all the resources at our disposal to address our reading goals. For example, as was customary for elementary schools in our district, we held what were called monitoring conferences. Their purpose was to track the prog-ress of all the students in each teacher's classroom and to form an action plan to deal with each and every individual. Reading was always front and center.

The monitoring questions were standard: How many kids were op-erating at basic, proficient, and advanced levels? Was there any reason that all of them couldn't be at least at a proficient level by the end of the year? If not, why not? Were there concerns about physical health? Did we have any reason to suspect that cognitive functioning was impaired? Was social-emotional adjustment an issue? What did we know about the families? Was there any history of abuse or neglect? Using the answers to these questions, we set goals and developed a list of interventions de-signed to meet them.

There was nothing extraordinary about any of this. The monitoring conference was standard operating procedure in the Milwaukee public schools, a district that was seen as a model of reform by many, and one that never ceased to remind us of our core mission to advance pupil achievement. A highly skilled cadre of staff development professionals provided ongoing training on a system-wide basis and made itself acces-sible to deal with the specific needs of individual schools as well. Its ap-proach to reading skills development reflected those constructivist ideals that stressed meaning and comprehension over part-to-whole strategies such as direct and systematic code-based training. There was nothing surprising about that. Most schools operated within that framework, one that reflected the kind of training provided by schools of education across the country.

I never doubted that philosophy nor deviated from it until late in my career when a young teacher named Gayle Gorman joined our staff. Gayle was a real dynamo, action-oriented, demanding yet nurturing, and a vi-brant force for student improvement. Early in the year, Gayle asked per-mission to use a program called *Reading Mastery*. She told me the approach was very different from what we were currently doing and that it would employ a systematic, drill-oriented emphasis of the alphabetic code.

What Gayle was suggesting, of course, was heresy. The word "drill" alone would normally squelch consideration of any program that used such a tactic. One could attempt to sanitize it, perhaps referring to it as a "tightly scaffolded" approach to skills development. But in the end, it was repetitive practice until one could demonstrate mastery. Such contrivances, I had always been taught, were antithetical to the very notion of child-centricity.

But Gayle had piqued my curiosity. Her group was comprised of second-graders losing ground in their efforts to read and comprehend. Only a few months out of first grade, they had already managed to amass significant deficits. As most educators will attest, such deficiencies tend to be cumulative, a condition that causes those who have them to become increasingly less proficient as they travel through the grades. This is harmful to all children, but nowhere is it more devastating than among victims of poverty and all its associated ills. Over 90 percent of the children in my school fell into that category and I knew I had both a professional and moral responsibility to them, regardless of their life circumstances. In fact, their impoverished status intensified that responsibility.

Normally, a group like Gayle's would generate a list of special interventions. For example, we might have suggested individual counseling for a student who had recently been placed in foster care. Or perhaps we would have done vision and hearing screening on a child who was exhibiting problems with visual and/or auditory discrimination. If necessary, we would develop individual behavior plans for those who chronically disrupted classroom proceedings or made a referral for a child with a suspected processing deficit.

But Gayle didn't mention any such issues. She simply had a group of below-level readers, and she felt strongly that she could turn things around. There were too many groups like Gayle's performing below acceptable thresholds. Perhaps it was time to try something different. Principals were always encouraged to take risks, to think outside the metaphorical box. If ever there was a time in my career to consider something radical, this was surely it.

But there were also other reasons to give serious consideration to Gayle's appeal. One had to do with expectations, and her swagger showed a confidence I rarely observed. The way Gayle saw it, the goal for every one of her second-graders, regardless of their current functioning, was for them to perform at their age-appropriate level by the end of the year. A year's progress in a year's time wouldn't cut it if they were more than a year behind to begin with. A deficit of any kind was simply unacceptable. When she was done with them, her second-graders would read like third-graders.

In addition, Gayle made no demands for additional support. More aide time would be nice, but, if it wasn't available, she'd make do. I observed the manner in which she interacted with her students and I couldn't bring myself to believe she would subject them to anything untoward. I decided to let her do her thing and see where it led.

NEW HOPE

By June, using the district's assessment tool to verify reading fluency
and comprehension, Gayle had succeeded in elevating all but one of her
twenty-two children to an age-appropriate level of proficiency. This was
a success rate of 95 percent. The following year, in third grade, those same
children scored proficient or advanced on the state's reading comprehension test. I was ecstatic and the kids were beaming, showing the kind of
self-esteem that comes only from success. I suddenly had more cause for
optimism than at any other time in my career, optimism that we could
begin reaching children we had failed so often in the past.

Gayle had indeed achieved impressive results with her students, but it
did not come as any surprise to her. In her mind, all she was doing was
following a specified set of procedures whose efficacy had been validated
through scientific testing. These measures called for direct, intensive, and
systematic treatment of the alphabetic code as a first step in learning to
read. If you taught children to master these concepts and applied them
in real text with consistency and with precision, children would advance,
incrementally but inexorably.

After several years, I can report that we did show progress, especially
where fidelity to the program was most in evidence. However, we never
replicated as a school the kind of success Gayle had been able to achieve
with her group. Obviously, there were reasons for this. Gayle was a skilled
practitioner and delivered the program with the grace and fluidity of a
piano virtuoso. In addition, she could deliver it under controlled conditions where little could come between her and the specified procedures
necessary to carry it out. Because there was only the one group, there were
few logistical problems. She had the materials she needed and, perhaps
most importantly, she had total faith in what she was doing.

STARK REALITY

It was one thing to elicit this kind of success under such conditions but
doing so more extensively was another matter. Most of our teachers
had been willing to give it a try, but support was never unanimous.
It was an especially tough sell at the kindergarten level where reading readiness rather than actual reading ability had always been the
developmentally appropriate goal. All this was understandable for a
number of reasons.

First, as has been stated, "direct instruction" used methods that were
anathema to just about everything teachers had ever been taught. As
a result, they would need to commit time and energy toward getting

training to deliver a program they didn't necessarily believe in. In addition, the specified practices called for by *Reading Mastery* meant teachers would lose much of the curricular autonomy they had always enjoyed in the past, thereby reducing the opportunity to inject their own creative instincts into the reading lesson. It was indeed a tenuous course upon which teachers were asked to embark, and I have nothing but praise for those who exhibited the courage to follow such a path.

But there were other obstacles toward implementation of such a program that went well beyond the local school. The overall climate was simply not favorable to such practices.

The very words I use to describe them—direct, intensive, systematic—were enough to cause allergic reactions among whole-language purists and others who purported to uphold the spirit of child-centrism. Such practices are generally not taught in schools of education and they are not stressed among staff development professionals, so it is little wonder they are not often practiced in classrooms.

When such methods attempt to nudge their way into districts, they are viewed with doubt and suspicion and seen as an incursion that violates holistic principles. Some questioned Gayle's results, maintaining they would not hold up over time and offered sundry other caveats:

- Children do not respond to drill-based practices.
- This is a "cookie-cutter" or "one-size-fits-all" program.
- Children might learn to decode, but they don't learn to comprehend.
- There might be research to back it up, but there is research to support just about anything.
- Students will lose motivation to participate in reading activities of any kind.

I tried to counter those arguments by expressing the opinion that direct and systematic treatment of the alphabetic code merited a rightful place on a long list of child-centered practices. That caused some to wonder whether fermentation had invaded my neurochemistry somewhat prematurely because, as several explained it to me, direct and systematic *anything* is antithetical to the spirit of child centricity. It was an oxymoronic relationship.

All this reflected the holistic climate that permeates schools of education across the country. These teacher preparation institutions grant diplomas, sign off on teacher license applications, and provide continuing education for practicing teachers. Needless to say, they have enormous influence on the manner in which early reading instruction is delivered, and a scripted, alphabetic program has been, and continues to be, persona non grata at most of them, regardless of what empirical evidence might suggest. In those venues, it appears as if such evidence doesn't exist or, if it does, it is to be viewed as an abomination, a threat to legitimate curricula.

I realize that comment will not ingratiate me with many education professors, but there is evidence to back it up. A recent study by the National Council on Teacher Quality found that reading science is conspicuous by its absence.[1] Perhaps that explains why the local university chose to remove its student teachers from my building after we adopted *Reading Mastery* and other direct instruction programs.

PASSIVE/AGGRESSIVE

The tension manifested itself in countless ways. For example, I had organized a staff development session on one of the days set aside on the school calendar for that purpose. In order to save money, I partnered with two other schools in arranging to have one large session at a site that could accommodate our combined staffs. As I said earlier, not everyone at my school fully supported RM, but I never encountered the kind of resentment I saw displayed by some others that day.

Two teachers plunked themselves near the exit and behaved like prepubescent teens, laughing and giggling and generally ignoring most of what was going on. They ignored me when I asked them to move forward to two of the many empty seats near the front and continued to banter about unrelated topics. Most other participants acted appropriately, but I did notice that several were reading newspapers while a few others were doing crosswords. One young man was nodding off and became angry when the presenter called on him to offer his views on what was being said. The other principals explained to me that these behaviors reflected the attitudes of some staff members who were disaffected by the incursion of a method they held in little regard and who were not above attempting to undermine, if not sabotage, its implementation.

My purpose in relating this incident is not to highlight the unprofessional conduct of a few. Those who behaved in this manner were probably decent individuals with good teaching records. They were merely expressing their derision for a program that bore little resemblance to how they had been trained and what was to be valued. Showing the efficacy of such an approach was not a message they were willing to accept under any circumstances. It was like asking a Christian fundamentalist to embrace the spirit of Allah.

The agitation between conflicting methods played itself out in other ways also. It strained relationships between staff development leaders and RM schools as the two vied for precious resources in an environment of shrinking revenues. I became especially aware of this when

I took on the role of principal-mentor for several schools attempting to maintain or initiate RM programs. As such, I frequently attended meetings to lobby district leaders for more dollars and more training opportunities for my clients and their staffs. Oftentimes, I found myself at odds with those who viewed my presence as emblematic of an attempt to compromise their holistic standards. Even though each side tried to conduct business in a professional manner, the tension was always palpable.

This was indeed an unfortunate circumstance, given that we shared a common goal and I would never claim that my resolve was in any way superior to that of anyone else. I was dealing with consummate professionals who were focused on the district's chosen curriculum. In that regard, they knew how to deliver it and how to communicate it to those less skilled and less experienced. The disconnect existed because the approach I used attempted to redefine—perhaps reinvent—the child-centric paradigm while theirs remained steadfastly loyal to the original version.

All these things tended to compromise our effort. But such is the case when forces oppose rather than facilitate one another. It seemed to be a battle of wills, a struggle between good and evil, between one person's science and another's. Did it really have to be that way? Wasn't there a middle ground on which the two constructs could meet and, thereby, synergize their efforts? On the surface, the answer would seem to be no, but I had a hard time accepting that premise. So, if it indeed were to be possible, I would have to look beneath the surface, try to identify those things that united us rather than drove us apart.

I began asking myself questions such as these:

- Did the use of a systematically scripted, code-based program represent an irreconcilable difference that could never be overcome?
- Had we really listened to one another and sought ways to accommodate and integrate divergent viewpoints?
- What did the data really say in regard to reading methodology?
- Was what many suggested true, that research could validate nearly any reading strategy?
- Is systematic phonics instruction antithetical to the spirit of a "child-centered" curriculum?
- Can systematic phonics peacefully coexist with holistic practices?
- What exactly do we mean by developmentally appropriate instruction?

These questions haunted me and I resolved to pursue my own truth in regard to them. I would do so by examining the history of the reading debates and analyzing the purest and most unassailable expressions of scientific evidence. All I needed was the time to investigate these matters deeply. That time had arrived.

NOTE

1. Walsh, Glaser, and Wilcox, Executive Summary, *What Education Schools Aren't Teaching about Reading and What Elementary Teachers Aren't Learning*, 4ff.

3

❦

Soporific Effluvium

"'Twas blow for blow, disputing inch by inch, For one would not retreat, nor t'other flinch."

—George Gordon Lord Byron, *Don Juan*

Direct instruction's *Reading Mastery* provided comprehensive treatment of the alphabetic code through specified teacher-directed practices, all of which were offensive to constructivist sensibilities. But that was but a means to an end. Once mastered, the need for alphabetic training disappeared and instruction could then focus exclusively on meaning-based activities. In other words, alphabetic mastery provided a gateway to a constructivist or whole-language world. It's kind of like attaining keyboard mastery. When an author need not concern himself with locating each letter, all his time can be devoted to the ideas he wishes to convey.

Despite the dualistic message it contains, that interpretation does not fit the holistic paradigm. Strict constructivists disavow the notion that inoculating children with a serum of direct and systematic code-based practices constitutes a legitimate path toward literacy. They would maintain that, if there is scientific evidence to the contrary, then there must be something wrong with the science. This attitude severely undermines the data and short-circuits attempts to accommodate divergent approaches. Meanwhile, literacy rates continue to languish and achievement gaps continue to widen, all at a time when such skills are more essential than ever.

To gain some insight into how we might have arrived at such a point, I decided to investigate the struggle between reading methodologies that has played itself out in this country since the mid 1800s. After having gone through that exercise, it no longer remained a mystery as to why the educational community has become so polarized in how it chooses to address one of the most significant public health issues of our day.

At times, the debates have been so rancorous as to reveal a pattern of undulating vitriol and Hulk Hogan–ish diatribes that would cause a sailor to blanch. Even to this day, the matter remains mired in a state of tension and disequilibrium marked by smug professionals behaving like snarling dogs looking to defend their territory by lashing out at unenlightened challengers with venomous attacks and spurious claims. That may seem like hyperbole, but it's not.

SOPORIFIC EFFLUVIUM AND GHOSTLY APPARITIONS

In this country, the struggle may have begun in New England in the 1840s. Back then, teachers brandished their instructional authority with the subtlety of a meat cleaver by literally brow-beating number facts and alphabetic knowledge into their quavering charges. Those who failed to sit still and chant the drills obediently, accurately, and unceasingly could expect various forms of extrinsic motivation. The harsh discipline included ridicule, corporal punishment, and other forms of what would today be considered physical and emotional abuse. It was a crude system that warranted change.

Such an opportunity arose when Horace Mann became secretary of the board of education for the Commonwealth of Massachusetts in 1839. Even though he did not have a background in education, Mann viewed his appointment as a mandate to recast the business of educating the state's children in a new and different mold. While Mann was on a trip to Europe, the director of Leipzig's schools, Dr. Charles Vogel, took him on a classroom tour. What struck Mann most was the dichotomous (compared to U.S. practice) manner in which children were taught to read.

> Not only did he . . . notice the exceptional quality of the teachers, but he paid great attention to the specific methods they employed. Instead of the children being expected to learn individual letters by rote memory, then syllables, and finally words, they were given books with pictures of common objects. Underneath each picture was its simple name.[1]

Mann found such tactics tailor-made to his progressive agenda that sought to foster literacy through kindness, respect, and various other expressions of what came to be known as a child-centered curriculum.

But if Mann was looking for a kinder and gentler approach, he chose not to apply that same measure of sensibility to those upon whom it would fall to carry it out. Shunning an opportunity for polite debate and wielding his position as secretary, he launched a series of attacks aimed at the teaching establishment in general and an association of Boston schoolmasters in particular. The bitter invective came via a series of annual reports to the Massachusetts Board of Education. At times, the language reads like that of a Stephen King novel. As chronicled by M. J. Adams:

> In his annual reports for the board of education, Mann decried the "odor and fungousness of spelling-book paper" from which "a soporific effluvium seems to emanate . . . steeping [the child's] faculties in lethargy."[2]

At one point during a lecture entitled "On the Best Mode of Preparing and Using Spelling Books":

> [He] caustically denounced alphabetic lists, referring to the letters in them as "skeleton-shaped, bloodless, ghostly apparitions, and hence, it is no wonder that the children look and feel so deathlike when compelled to face them."[3]

The tone of these remarks suggests that Mann had hired Edgar Allan Poe to ghostwrite them. (In fact, Poe and Mann were contemporaries, Poe having published "The Raven" in 1845.) Even so, one could argue that he (Mann) was trying to exercise some restraint given that there were other words he could have substituted for effluvium. But, in reality, Mann was in a state of intense agitation. He dismissed the schoolmasters' pupils' alphabetic accomplishments by maintaining, "A parrot or an idiot could do the same thing."[4]

That constituted a tipping point for the schoolmasters who now felt compelled to respond. As Mann's biographer, Jonathan Messerli, tells it:

> Finally moved to defend themselves, they fought back with a vehemence more typical of a blood feud, marshaling every verbal weapon of invective and scorn available, heretofore employed only upon their hapless pupils.[5]

In a response entitled, *Remarks on the Seventh Annual Report of the Hon. Horace Mann, Secretary of the Massachusetts Board of Education*, the schoolmasters sought "to correct erroneous impressions."[6] In so doing, they characterized Mann as an eccentric, aberrant purveyor of mindless reform. They contended that Mann's outrageous suggestion of abandoning the alphabet in favor of whole-word methods placed him squarely on the lunatic fringe. For good measure, they threw in a denunciation of Mann's innovative Normal Schools for teacher training as "propaganda agencies for his 'hot-bed theories,'" and accused him of exciting the prejudices of the ignorant.[7]

If anyone had taken the time to reflect on the effects this was having on Boston schoolchildren, perhaps cooler minds could have prevailed.

A thick skin would have served Mann well but such an attribute was not among his many admirable qualities. He took this challenge to his authority personally and, against the advice of his supporters, he lashed out with the even more inflammatory *Reply to the "Remarks" of the Thirty-one Boston Schoolmasters on the Seventh Annual Report of the Secretary of the Massachusetts Board of Education.*

According to Messerli, "Mann was here the polemicist, caustic, scornful, and severe." Mann called the schoolmasters selfish and absorbed reactionaries who confronted children with a perpetual fear of pain while casting himself as the "bearer of righteousness and the defender of justice." Messerli summed it up by suggesting that Mann was "urging more teaching and less flogging."[8]

The heat was now so intense that two of the schoolmasters deserted their colleagues and took refuge in the safety of their classrooms where they were once again free to take out their frustrations on their unfortunate charges. But the remaining twenty-nine prepared to do further battle. Pursuing yet again this game of one-upmanship, they issued a more than two-hundred-page *Rejoinder to the "Reply" of the Hon. Horace Mann; Secretary of the Massachusetts Board of Education to the "Remarks" of the Association of Boston Masters upon His Seventh Annual Report.* This document dealt in trivialities and essentially restated the schoolmasters' previous arguments, albeit in less volatile terms.

By this time, the exchanges were becoming repetitive and little more than an attempt to get the last word. Mann was too proud to allow that to happen and so launched yet another volley. This time, however, he would have a follow-up strategy. The first step was to counter any charges that impugned his professional judgment. He did this by issuing his *Answer to the "Rejoinder" of the Twenty-nine Schoolmasters, Part of the Thirty-one Who Published "Remarks" on the Seventh Annual Report of the Secretary of Massachusetts Board of Education.*

The coup de grace, though, was the second prong of Mann's attack, a New England version of "shock and awe." He mobilized his supporters on the Boston School Committee and let fly with the most feared of all weapons—the standardized test. Effluvium had truly hit the fan.

> Beginning early in the morning, as if armed with a search warrant, each man swooped down unexpectedly on a school and administered examinations the committee had written and privately printed. To be sure that the master in one school did not disclose the contents of the test to another, all schools were tested on the same subject on the same day.[9]

Educators today will appreciate the irony of that strategy being used by a liberal reformer to squelch his conservative opponents. In any case, the report was as one might expect, a repudiation of virtually everything that transpired daily in Boston classrooms. The results showed that students gained little in the way of practical knowledge other than the ability to perform rote memorization. What they did memorize was deemed useless and was said to have accomplished nothing other than to terrorize children by forcing them to interact daily with those skeleton-shaped, bloodless, ghostly apparitions.

The schoolmasters were, perhaps, duly chastened, although there is little evidence that the furor led to any immediate reforms. Once the effluvium settled, reading instruction returned to its phonics roots. It would take some seventy-five years for Mann's ideas to gain traction, but there is no question that he had set the stage for a migration from phonics and toward the principles of holism that dominate classroom practice today.

THE PROGRESSIVE MOVEMENT[10]

Progressives were bent on implementing measures that were seen as being more child-friendly or child-centric. That could be expressed in a variety of ways, but central to that purpose was the need for children to extract meaning from each and every one of their interactions with text. Alphabetic knowledge was at cross-purposes to this goal. Children could assign some understanding from their recognition of an entire printed word because of its familiarity in listening and speaking. But there was no such immediate value in knowing that *p* stands for the *puh* sound, for example. As Mann had declared earlier, a parrot or an idiot could be taught to do this.

The remedy, therefore, was to focus on whole words rather than their component parts. At one point, phonics instruction fell into such disfavor that Colonel Francis Wayland Parker, the superintendent of schools for Quincy, Massachusetts (1875–1883) and principal of Cook County Normal School in Chicago (1883–1889), thought it best to refrain from teaching alphabetic symbols "to prevent the child from becoming confused about the names and sounds of letters."[11]

William Gray was another pioneer in the whole-word movement. His *Curriculum Foundations* series (Scott Foresman) used intense, sustained, and systematic use of whole-word instruction and, in so doing, familiarized many of us with two of his ubiquitous characters, Dick and Jane. These readers presented new word lists at each level and built familiarity with them by repeated exposures in connected text: *See Dick run. See Jane run. See Dick and Jane run. Dick and Jane jump. Dick and Jane jump and run. See Dick and Jane jump and run.*

The irony here is that the continuous repetitions of words represented some of the same drill-oriented methods most frequently associated with alphabetic training. Gray was merely substituting repetitive words for repetitive parts of words. In addition, his measures were quite specified. Teacher manuals contained step-by-step instructions while little attention was given to the kind of discovery learning and divergent thinking espoused by progressive purists. Despite the less than perfect fit with holistic principles, Gray's readers and similar basals dominated reading instruction from the 1930s through the 1960s when progressivism underwent an evolutionary change from whole word to whole sentences, to whole books then, literally, to "whole-language."

Other key figures in the movement toward holism included John Dewey, G. Stanley Hall, and Edmund Burk Huey. Dewey, arguably the most famous educator in all American history, developed his Laboratory School at the University of Chicago as a way to test the viability of his recommendations for a broader and less-structured approach to curriculum. Hall maintained that schools did children a disservice by attempting to mold them based on preconceived adult goals. The expression "developmental appropriateness" would have appealed to Hall, who saw no reason to rush children into literacy. Children, he believed, would learn to read when they had a mind to do so.

In 1908, Huey wrote *The Psychology and Pedagogy of Reading*, a comprehensive analysis of meaning-based approaches. Huey's work became a flash point later in the century when opposing forces in the reading community began to collide. In spite of the controversy his work sparked, Huey's ideas had a significant influence on the training of both teachers and administrators throughout the United States, and, by 1920, whole-word approaches had pretty much replaced phonics as standard operating procedure in American classrooms. There may have been some who continued to teach mainly from an alphabetic perspective, but they were pretty much on their own since the last strictly phonics reader went out of print in the mid-1930s.

While many continued to debate issues pertinent to early-reading training during this time, I find it interesting that this progressive period did not precipitate the kind of ideological confrontations we saw when Mann first proposed his ideas. Perhaps it occurred so gradually that most educators were oblivious to its evolution. But another explanation might lie in the fact that the constructs of progressivism were difficult to oppose. Those who had the temerity to confront them ran the risk of being characterized as some sort of anti-child-centric or anti-meaning-based thug. For whatever reason, the arena of reading pedagogy from the 1920s through the mid-1950s was a period of relative calm, a *pax lectura*, as two experts later put it.[12] But that would all change in 1955.

THE WAY OF ALL FLESCH

The backlash to progressivism occurred when heretofore unknown patterns of reading failure began to emerge and parents began wondering why their children were incapable of sounding out the simplest of words. Enter Rudolph Flesch, who set about the task of sending the pendulum back from whence it came. The growling, vituperative Flesch launched a salvo of attacks on holistic principles in his best seller, *Why Johnny Can't Read*. In it, he accused the educational community of turning the clock back some 3,500 years by choosing to ignore the very reason alphabets were created in the first place.

Essentially, he was questioning the reasonableness of asking kids to memorize the specific contours of tens of thousands of separate entities when we could build independent word recognition ability with a mere forty-four symbols. Interestingly, Flesch used the same animal-training metaphor to denounce whole-word strategies as Horace Mann had employed to condemn alphabetic practices:

> It seems to me a plain fact that the word method consists essentially of treating children as if they were dogs. It is not a method of teaching at all; it is clearly a method of animal training. It's the most inhuman, mean, stupid way of foisting something on a child's mind.[13]

And if that wasn't enough to cause Flesch's neck to radiate with varying shades of crimson, there was also the progressive notion of "reading readiness" that recommended the withholding of formal reading instruction until children showed they were prepared to engage in such activities. Flesch charged that we squandered the entire kindergarten year waiting for kids to express an interest in learning to read. He believed this had more to do with adults than kids. Reading readiness, he maintained, "means the readiness of the *teacher* to let the child start reading."[14] He also referred sarcastically to "readiness" as the "holy of holies, the inner sanctum of the whole 'science' of reading."[15]

Flesch found this to be especially disabling for American children given that English has more phonetic symbols and more inconsistencies from normal letter patterns than do other languages. These two conditions—waiting for children to be ready for instruction and learning to deal with the discrepancies of normal letter patterns—put us two years behind other nations in preparing children in a critical skill and at a critical period in their development. Flesch did not want to ignore children's social and emotional needs, but he saw no reason why they could not be addressed in concert with reading instruction rather than in lieu of it. Flesch's book devotes several pages to dissertational research by Donald C. Agnew, Duke University, in 1939, and sums up the outcome in this way: "It's exactly as he says: If you want to teach children how to read, you need phonics; if you just want to make them feel good, you don't."[16]

Flesch's message resonated with the public and Johnny remained on the best-seller list for thirty-nine weeks. Phonics suddenly began getting more attention in schools, with publishers finding ways to inject it into their basal reading programs. But this was a short-lived phenomenon. The educational community closed ranks, referring to Flesch as "The Devil in the Flesch" and denouncing those who bought into his arguments as "Flesch Peddlers."[17]

But he himself was responsible for much of the backlash. In his narrative, he had been indiscriminate in his denunciations. In so doing, he had impugned the intellect and honesty of experts, accusing them of conspiring with one another, of being driven more by the profit motive than anything else. And, in the spirit of the day, he even suggested that the anti-phonics faction was in some way associated with communism.

Such extreme rhetoric served to characterize him as a crackpot in many circles, and progressive leaders were in no way intimidated. The uproar did cause some to circle the wagons and wait for the heat to subside. But when they finally emerged, they redoubled their efforts, broadening and refining their holistic message to an extent that might well have made Flesch curl into the fetal position and remain there forever.

NOTES

1. Messerli, *Horace Mann: A Biography*, 395.
2. Adams, *Beginning to Read: Thinking and Learning about Print*, 22.
3. Balmuth, *The Roots of Phonics*, 190.
4. Smith, *American Reading Instruction*, 78.
5. Messerli, *Horace Mann: A Biography*, 413.
6. Messerli, *Horace Mann: A Biography*, 414.
7. Messerli, *Horace Mann: A Biography*, 414.
8. Messerli, *Horace Mann: A Biography*, 417.
9. Messerli, *Horace Mann: A Biography*, 419.
10. Material in this section has been distilled from Balmuth, *The Roots of Phonics: A Historical Introduction*.
11. Balmuth, *The Roots of Phonics*, 195.
12. Snow and Burns in preface of Snow, Burns, and Griffin, eds., *Preventing Reading Difficulties in Young Children*, v.
13. Flesch, *Why Johnny Can't Read*, 126.
14. Flesch, *Why Johnny Can't Read*, 70.
15. Flesch, *Why Johnny Can't Read*, 69.
16. Flesch, *Why Johnny Can't Read*, 67.
17. *Time Magazine*, January 9, 1956, www.time.com/time/magazine/article/0,9171,866725,00.html.

4

⤟⥸

Preponderance
of the Evidence

"What is research, but a blind date with knowledge?"

—William Henry

Why Johnny Can't Read was not the most scholarly of works. Flesch did cite a few studies, but they were outdated and lacked scientific rigor. Even among those, I noted some discrepancies between what he claimed in *Johnny* and what the studies actually said. Still, Flesch was onto something.

During this period, whole-word methods reigned supreme. Whether it was Dick and Jane, or David and Ann, or Bobby and Sue, looking and jumping and seeing Spot run, whole-word methods were ubiquitous in American classrooms. Those may not have been the most entertaining of stories, but the progressive culture was fixated on a whole-to-part, child-centered milieu of strategies seeking to shield children from those "ghost-like apparitions" otherwise known as letters of the alphabet.

Many did just fine with that, but for the first time, observers like Flesch began to notice uncharacteristic patterns of reading failure. Previously, those who attended school normally went on to become proficient readers absent any extraordinary circumstances such as traumatic brain injury or neurological dysfunction.

Flesch noticed that students who had difficulty remembering complete words were unable to use phonics as a backup strategy. Absent that skill, they had to resort to picture clues, context clues, and outright guessing. For such children, not only had reading become a difficult and laborious task, but the lack of fluency also prevented them from focusing on meaning. The result was not just reading failure but school failure in general, since every other subject was contingent on reading ability. As Paolo Lionni and Lana Klass noted, "Somewhere along the line, our schools had lost the ability to routinely educate children and produce uniformly good results."[1]

The higher rates of reading failure, coupled with the ongoing feuds, spawned research efforts to resolve the matter once and for all. They would apply to reading science the same kind of scientific rigor used in other fields such as medicine and engineering, so as to identify those practices that led most directly to literacy acquisition. Each attempt sought to produce a knowledge base so expansive and so rigorously defended there would no longer be a need to argue.

But that would indeed be a challenge. Previously, reading research had relied heavily on observational data to identify best practices. Quantitative comparisons of actual achievement would need to take precedence over that type of research platform. These comparison studies would also need to reflect higher standards of methodological purity than had previously been the case. In addition, researchers would need to both review existing studies and generate new data of their own and do so to such an extensive degree so as to dwarf any previous initiatives. A study here or there might lead to some insight but represent only a small part of what needed to be an integrated whole. The hope was that massive compilations of legitimately derived data would ultimately lead to a *preponderance of evidence*, one so strong that no right-thinking individual could choose to ignore it.

THE RESEARCH SYNTHESIS

In order to create such a preponderance of evidence, this new research movement would rely on something called *research synthesis*.

A research synthesis deals with aggregate data. If one study involving sixty pupils in two classrooms found a positive and significant relationship between a given reading method and achievement, imagine how much more powerful such information would be if it were based on fifty studies that conducted 114 comparisons involving 750 students from a wide range of geographic regions and income levels.

An effective research synthesis required scrupulous attention toward determining which studies merited inclusion. Those that qualified were selected from among many others as best demonstrating rigid adherence to the most strident of scientific standards. From there, these "best-of-the-best" could then be subjected to something called meta-analysis, a process that could produce numeric comparisons based on a sample size exponentially greater than any one study could ever hope to achieve. Its efficacy is summarized thusly:

> The research synthesis offers a concise and practical means of summarizing a vast body of literature. In turn, this permits recommendations about the value of existing programs and translates this information into informative statements to guide future practice and research.[2]

This process of looking at huge compilations of aggregate data is what characterized the research movement that began in the wake of Flesch. The remainder of this chapter provides brief synopses of nine such efforts spanning five decades, beginning in 1967 and ending in 2008. The analyses include quotes taken directly from the reports, my own interpretations, and interpretations taken from book and magazine reviews.

I include these descriptions mainly to inform the reader. That might sound a little condescending in that this book was written mainly for educators who teach reading. If these reports were so momentous, would not all of us who spent our years preparing for and engaging in reading instruction already be quite familiar with them? If my career is in any way representative, the answer would simply be no.

I had a superficial awareness of a few, but I was completely oblivious to most. Of even greater significance, perhaps, is the fact that, never in my entire career, was I ever expected to carry out classroom activities that bore any resemblance to a large portion of what these studies contain. That is not something I am proud to admit. It just happens to be true. Forgive me if I am being presumptuous in assuming I am not alone in that regard.

Another reason for reviewing these major reports is to give the reader some perspective on the enormity of the effort and attention to detail that went into them. As indicated, a synthesis gives an aggregate picture of a large number of studies which, in turn, involves an even larger number of test subjects. Sample size is a key element in establishing statistical significance, and, therefore, on that basis alone, these reports deserve a better fate than the chilly reception given them by the reading community over the years.

Lastly, the research syntheses account for an important issue not previously given much attention in the popular literature: replication.[3] Replication refers to the ability of investigators to produce similar results in unique studies of the same phenomena. Replication is a crucial hallmark of science because it ensures that results of studies are not due to chance or the result of fraud or poor research designs.

Collections of studies that produce consistent findings, in contrast, provide strong evidence for the veracity of a set of conclusions. In all sciences, replication is the fundamental method through which knowledge grows. For this reason, research syntheses that show consistent results from rigorous but disparate studies constitute especially powerful evidence.

But it is more than just sample size, meta-analysis, and replication that lend so much credibility to these reports. Another key factor involves the lengths to which the researchers went to preserve scientific integrity. They spared no effort in their attempts to adhere to the most rigorous standards with regard to such things as experimental design, the presence of treatment and control groups, degree of randomness, preservation of parallel groupings, project oversight—all those things that bolster an experiment's credibility. Those studies that failed to meet these rigid criteria were summarily dismissed from inclusion in the analyses.

Some of the projects did not sponsor any new studies of their own but rather sought to look at what was currently available with the goal of reaching consensus in its overall interpretation. Those efforts, such as *Becoming a Nation of Readers*, sought input from researchers who represented a wide variety of philosophical and pedagogical backgrounds. This would allay the fears of those who might otherwise claim that a project represented a faction comprised of individuals with preconceived notions and/or methodological biases. The objective would be to identify areas of agreement upon which theorists could build, as opposed to a widening of the chasm that had thwarted meaningful dialogue in the past.

One could spend months, perhaps years, analyzing the findings of the major investigations contained in this chapter. But remarkably, it is possible to capture the essence of all nine in but a couple of sentences.

1. Students who master the correspondence between sound and symbol at early levels are more likely to acquire literacy ability and to advance to higher reading levels than those who don't.
2. The ability to combine phonemes so as to recognize unfamiliar words does not in itself represent literacy but is an essential tool in its attainment.

I know there are a million other things that can be said or concluded about the data, but that is essentially what I found. I encourage you, the reader—even challenge you—to read the reports and conclude otherwise.

MAJOR REPORTS ON EARLY READING: 1967–2008

Chall—*Learning to Read: The Great Debate* (1967)

In the mid-1960s, the United States Office of Education launched *The Cooperative Research Program in First Grade Reading Instruction (CRP)*. Its purpose was to fill the research gap by producing new and improved data streams. A planning committee for the project was convened; among its members was a professor from Harvard by the name of Jeanne Chall.

Chall was curious about the research that had been conducted up until that point and how it might compare with the new data that would be forthcoming from the *CRP*. She therefore decided to look at all the experimental studies that had been completed between 1910 and 1965. She knew that locating and compiling the results from such a wide period would be a daunting task and that her analysis would be suspect due to the methodological flaws that characterized much of the early work on the subject. But, when she was done, she would have consolidated and analyzed more outcome-based data on beginning reading than ever before.

Chall was interested in determining whether this aggregate data pointed in any particular direction and, if so, whether it would validate or contradict what was forthcoming from the *CRP*. Chall's final report would have the added texture of knowledge gained by visiting more than three hundred kindergarten and first and second-grade classrooms in the United States, England, and Scotland and analyzing the most frequently adopted basal-reading series that were available at that time.

The culmination of Chall's work was reported in 1967 in the first of three editions of *Learning to Read: The Great Debate*. In 1996, in the introduction to the third edition, she made these statements about the original project:

> Based on these analyses, I found that beginning readers learn better when their instruction emphasizes learning the alphabetic code, one that places first importance at the beginning on learning the relationship between letters and their sounds (that is, learning the alphabetic principle). They learn less well when taught by a meaning-emphasis, that is, one that emphasizes, at the very beginning, how to understand what is read.
>
> What distinguished the more effective beginning reading instruction was its early emphasis on learning the code. Instruction that focused, at the beginning, on meaning tended to produce less favorable results.
>
> The research also suggested that a code-emphasis was particularly beneficial for children at risk—children from low-SES families, children with suspected learning disabilities, children with below-average intelligence, and children for whom English is a second language.[4]

It is important to note that Chall's work did not disavow the need for seeking meaning while learning to read. Indeed, she took pains to point out that comprehending text was the ultimate goal. What she found was that phonic ability—while in itself not producing this result—nevertheless represented a fundamental tool for developing the capacity to read and understand. To give an analogy, the possession of a wrench does not guarantee that one can install or repair indoor plumbing, but it would be very difficult to do so without such a tool.

Chall was more than a little surprised by these findings. Her preconceived notions, if any, would probably have favored the kind of progressive measures that had dominated reading practice for so long. In fact, she found the data to be so counterintuitive to the conventional wisdom that she felt the need to refine her analysis. This time she narrowed her investigation so as to compare achievement between those who received more *direct and systematic* phonics instruction to those who were taught phonics in a less intensive and more incidental manner.

> By an overwhelming margin, the programs that included systematic phonics resulted in significantly better word recognition, better spelling, better vocabulary, and better reading comprehension at least through the third grade (where the availability of any data tapered off).
>
> Moreover, the advantage of systematic phonics—though a bit slower to kick in—was just as great, and perhaps greater, for children of lower-entry abilities or socioeconomic backgrounds as it was for those more ready and more privileged.[5]

The Great Debate went on to become a seminal resource in identifying the most effective reading practices. Two more editions, one in 1983 and one in 1996, found even greater correlations between phonics ability and overall reading achievement, especially among disadvantaged populations.

Yet, embarrassing as it is to admit, until I began writing this book, I had never heard of Jeanne Chall.

Bond and Dykstra—*The Cooperative Research Program in First-Grade Reading Instruction* (1967)

Whereas Chall looked at the composite results of many past research efforts that had been conducted independently of one another, Bond and Dykstra not only sought evidence that was new but that also showed consistency in design, methodology, and quality control. Program facilitators selected, from a large number of submissions, those that reflected the most rigorous adherence to matters such as degree of randomization, adequacy of sample size, and consistency among groups. In the end, only twenty-seven studies qualified from among seventy-six that applied.

Much as consumers do when making buying decisions, the *CRP* investigators wanted to make sure that they were comparing apples to apples. All groups were administered the same pre- and post-tests. The length of time devoted to applying the method would be the same, as would the length of time spent on data collection. Participants would be required to collaborate with one another to ensure that they collected common information relevant to teacher, pupil, and community characteristics.

The study sought answers to several questions, including which of the many approaches to initial reading instruction produced superior reading and spelling achievement at the end of first grade. The report's co-authors concluded:

> Results of the correlation analysis revealed that the ability to recognize letters of the alphabet prior to the beginning of reading instruction was the single best predictor of first-grade reading achievement. The analysis of methodology indicated that the various non-basal instructional programs tended to be superior to basal programs as measured by word recognition skills of pupils after one year of reading instruction.[6]

Marilyn Jager Adams observed:

> According to Bond and Dykstra's analyses, the approaches that, one way or another, included systematic phonics instruction consistently exceeded the straight basal programs in word recognition achievement scores. The approaches that included both systematic phonics and considerable emphasis on connected reading and meaning surpassed the basal-alone approaches on virtually all outcome measures.[7]

Another of Bond and Dykstra's conclusions addressed the issue of developmental readiness:

> The analysis of treatments according to level of readiness for reading revealed that no method was especially effective or ineffective for pupils of high or low readiness as measured by tests of intelligence, auditory discrimination, and letter knowledge.[8]

In other words, level of readiness was a non-factor and, therefore, it was not necessary for teachers to wait around until children indicated that they were prepared for directed reading activities. Whether students were overjoyed at the prospect or not didn't matter. They could still engage in these kinds of endeavors and benefit from them.

While these studies were based on superior scientific methodology compared to those included in Chall's work, their conclusions were pretty much the same. What is more, these results were not ephemeral. Six years later, Dykstra replicated the original study by examining fifty-nine more and concluded:

> We can summarize the results of sixty years of research dealing with beginning reading instruction by stating that early systematic instruction in

phonics provides the child with the skills necessary to become an independent reader at an earlier age than is likely if phonics instruction is delayed
or less systematic.[9]

These results struck a chord with an author named Samuel Blumenfeld,
who had been reporting on the phenomenon of eroding literacy rates
and trying to identify their causes. In his 1973 book, *The New Illiterates*,
Blumenfeld wrote:

> In the course of researching this book, I made a shocking, incredible discovery:
> that for the last forty years the . . . children of America have been taught to read
> by a method originally conceived and used in the early 1800s to teach the deaf
> how to read, an [experimental] method which has long since been discarded by
> the teachers of the deaf themselves as inadequate and outmoded. Yet, today,
> the vast majority of . . . American children are still being taught by this very
> method. The result has been widespread reading disability.[10]

My analysis of the literature and events in the aftermath of these two
research syntheses led me to believe that, while many schools may have
taken to heart what Chall and the Bond and Dykstra studies recommended, for the most part, reading practice across the country continued
much as it had previously. Progressivists went on the offensive, attacking
both Chall and the Cooperative Research Program studies for a host of in-
fractions even though both studies agreed with the holistic viewpoint that
deriving meaning from print was the ultimate goal in learning to read.

However, I could find no such aggregate comparison data to undermine the efficacy of code-based knowledge nor to validate the kind of
holistic practices then in vogue. Despite the massive scope of the two
investigations, it was obvious that conventional practice was not going to
change. More data would be required.

Project Follow Through (Early 1970s)[11]

Project Follow Through was an offshoot of the federal Head Start Project. Despite the countless dollars spent to help disadvantaged children
overcome early learning deficits, a disturbing pattern had been noted.
Program evaluators found that any initial gains derived through Head
Start dissipated as soon as children left the program. And so Head Start
diverted its attention toward finding out whether there were any specific
programs that led to initial and sustained academic growth.

Follow Through looked at learning packages put together by teaching
teams, curriculum planners, publishers, etc. If one wanted to know which
practices were most essential for reading achievement, he or she would
need to look at the programs themselves to see what they contained.

The study looked at twenty-two instructional models categorized into three groups—a basic skills approach, a cognitive or conceptual model, and programs that emphasized a child's affective domain. The results were not fuzzy. Basic skills models produced the highest rates of achievement. And within that category, one stood out as superior to the others: direct instruction. Cognitive and affective models showed little correlation between their respective programs and literacy ability. In fact, one of the programs produced a negative relationship. In other words, if you used *that* program, your kids did *worse*.

I am not going to claim that this study trumps all others and that one need look no further for a high-quality reading program. But what I do know is, of the models included for analysis in Project Follow Through, those that employed direct and intensive phonics instruction were found to be significantly more effective than those that didn't.

This is what Rudolph Flesch, using a communication style similar to a primordial shriek, had tried to assert fifteen years earlier. This is what Chall had found and reported in *The Great Debate* and what Bond and Dykstra had determined in the Cooperative Research Program studies. The clear and consistent message I derived from this rapidly expanding database was this: there is intrinsic value in teaching children the relationship between sound and symbol and the best way to foster this skill in new readers is through direct, intensive, and systematic instruction of the alphabetic code.

Pflaum, Walberg, Karegianes, and Rasher—*Reading Instruction: A Quantitative Analysis* (1980)

Unlike the Cooperative Research Program and Project Follow Through, this research project was not looking to produce any new evidence. Instead, and more in the spirit of Chall's work, Susanna Pflaum and her associates sought to gather existing data from all the studies that had merited inclusion in the International Reading Association's *Annual Summary of Investigations Relating to Reading* between 1965 and 1978. These comparison studies were based on masses of data gathered through formal experimental procedures and scrutinized using relatively sophisticated statistical techniques. Their conclusions reflected the composite analysis of ninety-seven separate studies representing a total of 341 statistical comparisons.

The meta-analysis revealed that:

- Treatment groups outperformed control groups by a whopping average gain of twenty-three percentile points. In other words, programs subjected to intense scrutiny did better regardless of what strategies they employed.

- Higher gains were extracted from those treatments that lasted the longest.
- Children did better when teachers advocated for the interventions they were delivering to their students.[12]

I saw this as ammunition for those who maintained that one could find research to support nearly anything. All you had to do was study it.

In any case, the synthesis was not restricted to any specific intervention and, therefore, it had a difficult time finding in favor of any particular one. However, there was a notable exception:

> One specific treatment, sound-symbol blending, made a significantly greater impact on reading than the other experimental treatments. . . . With the different techniques for synthesizing research used in this study, this support for systematic phonics appears to be a strong one.[13]

An analysis of Pflaum's work prompted Adams to conclude:

> There was but one single class of instructional methods that resulted in gains significantly larger than any of the others. This class of methods consisted in teaching students about letters and letter sounds, first separately and then blended together. It consisted, in short, of explicit, systematic phonics.[14]

Once again, another major research compilation corroborated earlier findings, findings that validated elements from both sides of the reading debates.

Anderson, Hiebert, Scott, and Wilkinson, eds., *Becoming a Nation of Readers: The Report of the Commission on Reading* (1985)

The critical role of phonics in early literacy training had, by this point, been clearly established. It was no longer a matter of whether phonics should be taught, but rather how it should be taught.

Nevertheless, while skirmishes were still being waged in the research community and in both the professional and popular literature, reading failure continued to spiral out of control, and there was little evidence that phonics was getting the attention it merited. Adding to a burgeoning and already massive research base would serve little purpose.

Therefore, the organizers of the initiative that produced *Becoming a Nation of Readers* (BNR) proposed a different approach. They would get experts representing multiple disciplines and diverse viewpoints into the same room at the same time, allow them to ponder the evidence gathered over the past twenty years, and not let them emerge until they could produce a report with which they could all agree. Once that was done, they would communicate the results far and wide in the hope of establishing a cohesive reading policy to guide educators across the country.

In one respect, it seemed impossible that they could pull this off. After all, two decades of serious and comprehensive efforts to end the conflict had failed to resolve these differences. Ideologues merely attacked whatever evidence was not in alignment with their beliefs. *BNR* wasn't going to allow that. Each viewpoint would be given the kind of professional consideration it deserved.

I found this to be a form of educational conflict resolution, the kind of strategy we train kids to use to sort out their differences and improve the quality of their social interactions. Perhaps through that act of collaboration, participants would come to realize that, despite their philosophical preferences, there was as much to unite them as drive them apart. Wider discernment of these commonalities had the potential to create a win-win situation for both educators and kids. Only the most intractable of ideologues would choose to undermine such a cooperative venture.

The panel worked diligently to form a report that accommodated each position without compromising anyone's standards. It would appear that it succeeded as Chall, a panel member, indicated in the report's afterword:

> It is . . . a remarkable synthesis of the vast recent research on reading, which too often seems to have conflicting and controversial findings. The Commission members were appointed, in fact, to represent some of these differing viewpoints in reading, and our long and lively discussions would, in themselves, make a fascinating story.[15]

Becoming a Nation of Readers had recommendations for all stakeholders—parents, teachers, school boards, schools of education, etc. I could only find one of those recommendations that was even remotely controversial, that having to do with how best to foster reading readiness in children attending kindergarten.

Knowledge of letters and sounds, the report contends, is a superior way to build readiness and should not be sacrificed for traditional kindergarten activities such as cutting with scissors, pasting, coloring, and identifying geometric shapes. Those activities most certainly have a place in kindergarten classrooms, but their relationship to literacy development is tenuous at best. Reading readiness is better obtained through developmental reading activities, and children that age are quite capable of engaging in them without any loss of motivation or esteem.

Other suggestions included encouragement for the role of parents in supporting their children's literacy experiences, the need for teachers to maintain stimulating, disciplined, and print-rich environments, and advice to district administrations to lengthen and improve teacher education programs. Only two of the recommendations made specific reference to phonics:

> Teachers of beginning reading should present well-designed phonics instruction. Phonics is more likely to be useful when children hear the sounds associated with most letters both in isolation and in words and when they are taught to blend together the sounds of letters to identify words.[16]

> Classroom research shows that, on the average, children who are taught phonics get off to a better start in learning to read than children who are not taught phonics. . . . The picture that emerges from the research is that phonics facilitates word identification and that fast, accurate word identification is a necessary but not sufficient condition for comprehension. . . . Thus, the issue is no longer, as it was several decades ago, whether children should be taught phonics. The issues now are specific ones of just how it should be done.[17]

Those words are remarkably similar to what Chall found back in 1967:

> It should be noted that in reading, *both* meaning and the use of the alphabetic principle are essential. To read, one needs to be able to use *both* the alphabetic principle and the meaning of words.[18]

M. J. Adams—*Beginning to Read: Thinking and Learning About Print* (1990)

In the wake of *Becoming a Nation of Readers*, the Department of Education renewed its efforts to elicit new studies on the role of systematic phonics. As before, it sought new evidence to confirm previous findings. But it also wanted to go a step further by looking into the why and how—*why* phonics worked and *how* best to implement it in classrooms. The Center for the Study of Reading (CSR) agreed to "take on a major report that would thoroughly review all aspects of phonics and early reading instruction in a straightforward, evenhanded way."[19]

The culmination of this four-year investigation was Marilyn Jager Adams's *Beginning to Read: Thinking and Learning About Print*, written in collaboration with the CSR's panel of experts, representing diverse fields of study and various and sundry philosophical and methodological perspectives.

There is much detail to be examined in the conclusions drawn by Adams and communicated in *Learning to Read*. Again, my role has always been one of a practitioner and, therefore, a full understanding of all the intricacies that led to the final product may have eluded me. However, I found little equivocation in its overriding messages: systematic instruction in the alphabetic code facilitated children's ability to spell and recognize words and there exists a strong link between a thorough understanding of sound-symbol correspondence and the ease with which a child learns to read. As Adams states:

> The findings reviewed in Part II are suggestive of the conclusion that something about that large and general class of programs that purport to teach phonics is of genuine and lasting value. In particular, each of these categories of evidence suggests that students must appreciate the alphabetic principle to become proficient readers. They must acquire a sense of the correspondences between letters and sounds upon which it is based.[20]

What I took from Adams's message is that instantaneous processing of speech sounds is a vibrant impetus for word recognition, a force that kicks it into warp speed. The automaticity that eventually evolves allows one to process sounds without actually being consciously aware of having done so. When decoding ability reaches this level, more time and attention can then be given to the interrelationships among words, sentences, and paragraphs. This allows the reader to spend more time on the true reason for reading—to derive meaning from the text—to comprehend, literally, inferentially, associatively, to the very top rung of Bloom's taxonomy.

This all seems to make sense (again, in my opinion) when viewed in practical terms. Children come to school with both a speaking and a hearing vocabulary. Those who can sound out words are therefore likely to recognize them the second they do so, since they have both heard and spoken those words on countless occasions. What is heard, and its correspondence to what appears on the printed page, triggers an instant understanding of what they know from experience. The faster this process can occur, the faster it can be applied to whole bodies of text. The relationship between decoding and understanding is symbiotic, not contradictory.

True to her purpose, Adams also focused on how the alphabetic code should be taught. Constructivist theory indicated that the identification of the correspondence between sound and symbol was a natural outgrowth of interaction with text and, therefore, there was no need to teach it in any directed or skills-based way. That ran contrary to the research's message regarding direct and systematic instruction. According to Adams:

> Research indicates that regaining conscious awareness of the phonemic structure of speech is among the most difficult and critical steps toward becoming a reader. Importantly, research also indicates that children's awareness of phonemes can be hastened through appropriate training—and that such training produces significant acceleration in their acquisition of reading and writing skills.[21]

It is that acceleration I find so important. As stated earlier, the sooner one learns to unlock the alphabetic code, the sooner one can go about the business of deriving meaning from print. If direct and systematic teaching can hasten that process, why omit it or diminish its role in school curricula? I know of no one who would recommend a return to the practices of the nineteenth-century Boston schoolmasters, but some direct and systematic teaching given in measured daily doses would certainly seem appropriate given Adams's findings and those of her predecessors. If you truly want children to make the most of those print-rich environments, teach them to decode the words.

Snow, Burns, and Griffin, eds., Committee on the Prevention of Reading Difficulties in Young Children—*Preventing Reading Difficulties in Young Children* (1998)

More than thirty years had elapsed since Chall first "sought to understand why there had been such consistent controversy in the United States on teaching beginners to read."[22] Three decades of data collection and analysis revealed remarkably consistent findings, findings that validated diverse ways to bring about improvement. And yet the wars still raged, and no consistent effort was made to incorporate the scientific data into American classrooms. The 1998 report of the Committee on the Prevention of Reading Difficulties in Young Children, approved by the National Research Council (NRC) and supported by the National Academy of Sciences and the U.S. Department of Education, represented yet another effort to resolve the matter. As stated in the preface:

> The study reported in this volume was undertaken with the assumption that empirical work in the field of reading had advanced sufficiently to allow substantial agreed-upon results and conclusions that could form a basis for breaching the differences among the warring parties.[23]

The authors believed there was no longer a need to waste precious energy arguing about the efficacy of any given program or strategy. Reading levels had remained stagnant and achievement gaps became more expansive. This condition, in the context of increased demands for literacy, posed a serious public health issue, the implications of which were as much a threat to society as mumps, measles, smallpox, and rubella. The entire matter drew the attention of cabinet-level agencies and ultimately led to the formation of the Committee on the Prevention of Reading Difficulties in Young Children, an arm of the National Research Council. The hope generated by the ever-evolving research base was that children at risk could learn to read as well as their better-situated peers.

It was time to stop debating the matter and to apply the most effective practices highlighted in the data. Doing so would go a long way toward preventing reading deficits before they surfaced and give kids the best shot at meeting the advanced literacy requirements of an ever-growing technological society, one that suddenly found itself competing with new markets around the world. This report sought to improve reading instruction for all children, with special emphasis on those whose socioeconomic status, processing deficits, limited English proficiency, lack of preschool opportunity, etc., represented major obstacles to literacy attainment. Such individuals were disparately impacted because they had fewer support systems to aid them in overcoming instructional gaps. Failure to adequately prevent such gaps meant they were that much more likely to produce offspring with similar deficits and, as a result, replicate the same pattern of failure.

Most of what was contained in this report was yet another restatement of earlier findings. Children need to understand that letters and phonemes represent sounds and they also need to learn how to combine those individual entities to form words. However, these skills are irrelevant unless the children also have ample opportunity to see their application in connected text. From there it follows that children should have continuous opportunities to read throughout the day, whether in groups, with partners, independently, in content areas, for pleasure or information, or in any other conceivable context.

Having gotten to this stage of the research continuum, all that sounded to me like a broken record.

However, the NRC report was unique in that it identified five specific and critical elements that schools must address if they were to guarantee their pupils' literacy advancement: phonemic awareness, phonics, fluency, vocabulary, and comprehension.[24]

Preventing Reading Difficulties did not contend that there was one, and only one, way to go about building reading ability nor did it disavow the unique needs of each and every individual. But it did take into consideration the commonalities that existed among children. The cognitive functioning of students in a particular grade could be wide ranging but the majority could operate within specified parameters. Consequently, a significant proportion of students in a class could benefit from similar instructional dynamics and it made sense to take advantage of those common elements to address the needs of several rather than trying to do it one at a time.

Again, this made sense to me. All I ever heard was that each child should be treated as an individual and instruction should be tailored to each pupil. But is it feasible to expect that teachers can plan specific lessons for each child, each day? That has always been the expectation, and you would probably have a hard time getting any educator to admit that he or she didn't do just that. But if that were truly the case, why were schools organized by age and grade and why were basal readers and textbooks designed specifically for each developmental level?

The report of the National Reading Panel (NRP) two years later would base its objectives on the major findings summarized in *Preventing Reading Difficulties* and, thereby, drive reading policy during the transition from the Democratic administration of Bill Clinton and throughout George W. Bush's two terms as president. In fact, No Child Left Behind was launched with the stated goal of using these research findings as the criteria by which education funding would be allocated in the future.

National Reading Panel—*Teaching Children to Read: An Evidence-Based Assessment of the Scientific Research Literature on Reading and Its Implications for Reading Instruction* (2000)

As stated above, this report would draw upon its predecessor by targeting for study those critical elements identified by *Preventing Reading Difficulties in Young Children*. Those included alphabetics (phonemic awareness and phonics), fluency, vocabulary, and comprehension. (The report also dealt with teacher training and classroom technology but, as they are not directly pertinent to my topic, I will not report on those findings.) The goal was to add another dimension to the NRC's review of the literature. Whereas *Preventing Reading Difficulties in Young Children* had focused on the "what" (critical skills, environments, and early developmental interactions), the report of the National Reading Panel would use that information to concentrate on the "how" (the best ways to integrate the data into classroom practice). In pursuit of those goals, the panel:

- sought input from teachers, parents, administrators, policy makers, and other stakeholders through five regional hearings
- established a subgroup to review the literature for each of the five critical elements in early reading as identified by the NRC report
- considered only those studies that demonstrated the highest of research standards (to merit inclusion, studies had to report achievement results in quantifiable terms that were statistically different from the control group and no studies would be accepted unless they had been selected for publication in a refereed journal)
- used an experimental or quasi-experimental design that included a control group or multiple baseline method[25]

The panel felt strongly that children's learning needs, especially with regard to learning to read, were as important as their health-care needs and merited the same kind of methodology and standards as were used in medical research. Studies had to provide:

- a full description of all test subjects including demographics and cognitive, academic, and behavioral characteristics
- a full description of the specific treatment under investigation
- a report on the degree of fidelity to the research design and implementation
- a complete description of all outcome measures[26]

The final report of the NRP is significant not only for its resolute attention to its stated goals, but also for the sheer breadth of its investigation. First, researchers examined the various public databases and found they included over one hundred thousand studies on the subject of reading. Then they excluded any that did not specifically address the panel's targeted subjects (i.e., alphabetics, fluency, comprehension, teacher education, and technology). From there, each subgroup developed criteria that were similar to one another, yet varied enough to allow them to be specific to their respective topics. The panel of fourteen consisted of "leading scientists in reading research, representatives of colleges of education, reading teachers, educational administrators, and parents."[27]

In terms of sheer numbers, the panel considered tens of thousands of studies on the topics deemed most essential to early reading acquisition, subjecting them to a rigid screening process that reduced that number to some 417 individual experiments.

I counted 226 references in the alphabetics section alone. That chapter reported on 134 comparisons from ninety individual studies, all of which were included in the meta-analysis.

Below are the panel's findings with regard to the elements responsible for most of the debate that continued to fuel the reading wars—phonemic awareness and phonics:

- Phonemic awareness training helps children learn to read, spell, and comprehend.[28]
- Phonemic awareness helps students from many groups, including kindergartners and those most at risk of reading failure in the future.[29]
- Systematic phonics instruction makes a more significant contribution to children's growth in reading than do alternative programs providing unsystematic or no phonics instruction.[30]
- Phonics instruction taught early proved much more effective than phonics instruction introduced after first grade.[31]

- Phonics instruction produced substantial reading growth among younger children at risk of developing future reading problems.[32]
- Systematic phonics instruction produced significantly greater growth than non-phonics instruction in younger children's reading comprehension.[33]
- Systematic phonics instruction contributed more than non-phonics instruction in helping kindergartners and first-graders learn to spell.[34]
- Systematic phonics instruction is beneficial to students regardless of their socioeconomic status.[35]

The NRP also noted:

It is important to emphasize that systematic phonics instruction should be integrated with other reading instruction to create a balanced reading program. Phonics instruction is never a total reading program. . . . Phonics should not become the dominant component in a reading program, neither in amount of time devoted to it nor in the significance attached.[36]

The NRP found that researchers had not paid attention to motivational factors for both students and teachers and that there was "common agreement that fluency develops from reading practice."[37] Further, the report says:

Fluency is an essential part of reading and the NRP has reviewed its theoretical and practical implications for reading development. In addition, the Panel has conducted two research syntheses, one on guided oral reading procedures such as repeated reading and the other on the effect of procedures that encourage students to read more. These two procedures have been widely recommended as appropriate and valuable avenues for increasing fluency and overall reading achievement.[38]

I have chosen to focus on the phonetic component of the NRP report mainly because, as we have seen, that aspect is what is so often disregarded in classrooms. But as was the case in all the previously cited reports, there is much in it for a whole-language purist to love. The alphabetic component comprises but a fraction of the total, the remaining topics being devoted to vocabulary, comprehension, teacher training, and the use of technology for reading instruction. This can be verified in seconds by simply downloading the report of the subgroups at www.nationalreadingpanel.org/Publications/subgroups.htm.

Despite such a massive and skillful attempt to get at the truth, the final result was much as Chall had found some thirty-three years earlier. We weren't learning much that we didn't already know. But that didn't prevent us from ignoring that knowledge to a large extent. Certainly, phonics was getting more attention than it had in the past, but it wasn't being implemented in the manner recommended by massive compilations of data. Why not?

National Institute for Literacy—*Developing Early Literacy: Report of the National Early Literacy Panel; A Scientific Synthesis of Early Literacy Development and Implications for Intervention* (2008)

The National Early Literacy Panel (NELP) sought to analyze and synthesize scientific research on the development of early literacy ability of children ages zero to five. As was the case with its predecessor, the National Reading Panel, the NELP convened a group of experts from diverse fields of study including reading, early literacy, language, cognition, English as a second language, pediatrics, special education, research methodology, and early childhood education. The panel poured through some eight thousand experiments and screened them for research relevancy and methodological rigor. When they were done, they had identified five hundred research articles for inclusion in the meta-analysis.

But the group faced a special challenge in attempting to identify the best ways to go about building reading ability in children so young. The vast majority of preschoolers do not acquire conventional literacy skills such as decoding ability, oral fluency, and comprehension until after they begin formal schooling. This is true even in kindergarten, where, as we have seen, readiness to acquire these skills has long been the developmentally appropriate goal. In light of this, the NELP could not draw statistical comparisons between reading interventions and manifestations of these abilities in such young children since, even under the best of circumstances, they are not likely to possess them.

To deal with that conundrum, the NELP analyzed research to determine those precursor skills that were most highly correlated or predictive of later literacy attainment. The top five most closely related to future literacy attainment were: alphabetic knowledge, phonemic awareness, the ability to rapidly name letters, objects, and colors, the ability to write letters in isolation, and the ability to remember spoken information.[39]

Having established those criteria, the panel then went about the task of determining which strategies were most likely to produce that preemergent skill set. Five such interventions were identified: code-focused interventions, shared reading interventions, parent and home programs, preschool and kindergarten programs, and language enhancement programs.[40]

Code-based practices were found to "yield a moderate to large effect on the predictors of later reading and writing."[41] The panel found value in the other interventions also but expressed them in less expansive terms. For example, preschool programs had a large impact on preparing children for school[42] and shared reading experiences helped youngsters develop a facility for oral language and print.[43]

The NELP findings underscore the value of what parents do with their children prior to the time they enter into formal schooling. One cannot overestimate how much they benefit from the bedtime renditions of all of those ABC books—for example, adult and child alike basking in the joy of Dr. Seuss, pointing to the pictures, stressing the initial consonants: "Big B, little b, What begins with B? Barber, baby, bubbles, and a bumblebee."[44] But on the other hand, these results remind us of the deprivation of children who rarely get to engage in those kinds of prereading experiences.

A LOST OPPORTUNITY

In the new millennium the data stream continued to support what Chall had found in 1967, yet little regard was given to the ever-burgeoning knowledge base. Phonics may have been getting more attention than it had in the past, but not to the degree nor with the specificity suggested by the research. It appeared as though reading educators were spurning one opportunity after another to rally around data that accommodated their combined interests. The following chapter will attempt to shed some light on the reasons for this state of affairs.

NOTES

1. Lionni and Klass, *The Leipzig Connection*.
2. Cooper and Reach, "What Is a Meta-analysis and How Do We Know We Can Trust It?," in *The Voice of Evidence*, 123.
3. Jeff Lucas (associate professor and director of graduate studies, Department of Sociology, University of Maryland), telephone conference, July 22, 2008.
4. Chall, *Learning to Read: The Great Debate* (3rd ed.), n.p.
5. Adams, *Beginning to Read*, 38.
6. Bond and Dykstra, "The Cooperative Research Program in First-Grade Reading Instruction," 5.
7. Adams, *Beginning to Read*, 42.
8. Bond and Dykstra, "The Cooperative Research Program in First-Grade Reading Instruction," 5.
9. Dykstra, "Phonics and Beginning Reading Instruction," 397.
10. Blumenfeld, *The New Illiterates*.
11. Material in this section has been distilled from Snow, Burns, and Griffin, eds., *Preventing Reading Difficulties in Young Children*, 175–76.

12. Pflaum, Walberg, Karegianes, and Rasher, "Reading Instruction: A Quantitative Analysis," 14, 17.

13. Pflaum, Walberg, Karegianes, and Rasher, "Reading Instruction: A Quantitative Analysis," 18.

14. Adams, *Beginning to Read*, 48.

15. Anderson, Hiebert, Scott, and Wilkinson, *Becoming a Nation of Readers*, 123.

16. Anderson, Hiebert, Scott, and Wilkinson, *Becoming a Nation of Readers*, 118.

17. Anderson, Hiebert, Scott, and Wilkinson, *Becoming a Nation of Readers*, 37–38.

18. Chall, *Learning to Read*, n.p.

19. Pearson, "Foreword" in Adams, *Beginning to Read*, v.

20. Adams, *Beginning to Read*, 29.

21. Chall, *Learning to Read*, 412.

22. Chall, *Learning to Read*, n.p.

23. Snow and Burns in preface of Snow, Burns, and Griffin, eds., *Preventing Reading Difficulties in Young Children*, v.

24. Snow, Burns, and Griffin, eds., *Preventing Reading Difficulties in Young Children*, 6.

25. National Reading Panel, *Teaching Children to Read*, Reports of the Subgroups, 1–5ff.

26. National Reading Panel, *Teaching Children to Read*, 1–6.

27. National Reading Panel, *Teaching Children to Read*, 1–1.

28. National Reading Panel, *Teaching Children to Read*, 2–40 and 2–41.

29. National Reading Panel, *Teaching Children to Read*, 2–41.

30. National Reading Panel, *Teaching Children to Read*, 2–92.

31. National Reading Panel, *Teaching Children to Read*, 2–93.

32. National Reading Panel, *Teaching Children to Read*, 2–94.

33. National Reading Panel, *Teaching Children to Read*.

34. National Reading Panel, *Teaching Children to Read*, 2–94 and 2–95.

35. National Reading Panel, *Teaching Children to Read*, 2–95.

36. National Reading Panel, *Teaching Children to Read*, 2–136.

37. National Reading Panel, *Teaching Children to Read*, 2–92 and 2–137.

38. National Reading Panel, *Teaching Children to Read*, 3-28.

39. NELP, *Developing Early Literacy*, vii.

40. NELP, *Developing Early Literacy*, viii–ix.

41. NELP, *Developing Early Literacy*, 118.

42. NELP, *Developing Early Literacy*, 198.

43. NELP, *Developing Early Literacy*, 162.

44. *Dr. Seuss's ABC*, 6–8.

5

⊂∞⊃

Uniformity Unhinged

"'I don't see much sense in that,' said Rabbit.
'No,' said Pooh humbly, 'there isn't. But there was going to be when I began it. It's just that something happened to it along the way.'"

—A. A. Milne, *Winnie the Pooh*

There will be those, I am sure, who will contend I was selective in the reports I chose for inclusion in the previous chapter. They would be right; I was quite selective. I chose research syntheses instead of individual studies. In so doing, I was assured I would be looking at the aggregate results of huge compilations of data based on the highest degree of scientific rigor and analyzed by leading experts whose reputations were beyond reproach. I challenge anyone to identify sources that can compare in quality and scope to these massive efforts and that come to conclusions other than the ones they reached.

Having made this declaration, I will be categorized by some in the reading community as favoring only research-based strategies, the implication being that this is somehow a bad thing. My contention that reading science offers as much hope to students as medical science does to patients will be criticized as misguided and naïve. This chapter will take issue with that premise and attempt to show that ignoring such resolute and voluminous data represents a wholesale abandonment of our promises to do right by Johnny and his peers.

Those words may not sound magnanimous and accommodating to the various reading factions. Indeed, try as I might, I find it impossible to refrain from taking aim at a few who have succeeded in both sabotaging

51

and obfuscating the work of many. In the end, however, I hope I will have made a case that can appeal to the vast majority of educators who have never lost sight of their ultimate goal, and who are willing to keep an open mind and modify their practices in order to achieve it.

A DREAM DEFERRED

Each major report provided a window of opportunity to fuse alphabetic and holistic practices. Each recommended a code-based foundation that would enable children to participate and flourish in a constructivist world. And each afforded reading theorists the chance to lay petty differences aside and unite in pursuit of a common goal. The data were so powerful and offered such a cohesive message that it strains credulity to think that there would be those who would choose to castigate it.

But old habits die hard, especially among those who tend to operate well outside the mainstream. They pursue their agendas to such an exclusive degree that the road leading to ideology is their only logical choice. Having crossed into that realm, they are then willing to stifle anything they deem as a threat to their dogmatically derived versions of truth. Rarely does it ever occur to them that perhaps their insular positions are doing more harm than good and that it might be in everyone's best interest to seek common ground and unite on Johnny's behalf.

Nevertheless these immoderates continue to maintain their exalted positions. They are able to remain firmly entrenched atop their ivory towers, perceived by many as gurus, swamis with mystical powers that can transcend science, or redesign it in their own images. Those with the temerity to oppose them run the risk of banishment to a nuclear winter of political inexpediency.

How does this all come about? My examination of events revealed that reading ideologues employ several strategies to keep the light of experimental research from shining on American classrooms.

STRATEGY #1: UNDERMINE THE SCIENCE

Since constructivists could not stanch the endless stream of data that continued to validate the need for alphabetic training, they resorted to various expressions of plausible deniability. One was to question the ability of investigative science to draw legitimate comparisons, and to denounce those who engaged in such ventures.

The data that favored code-based practices were developed through an experimental, as opposed to an observational, research platform. This is the same kind of research used in medicine to determine the effectiveness of a particular treatment, such as reducing sodium intake or using a drug to control blood pressure. Some claimed such research was limited in its effectiveness to identify best practices for the teaching of reading. Classroom observations, anecdotal records, and teacher and pupil surveys, they maintained, were more appropriate in such a context.

For me, this begged the question as to why those supposedly trained in the scientific method would have such little regard for outcome-based valuations of performance, the only kind of evidence that deals with quantifiable measures of actual achievement. It also caused me to wonder why they would seek to *replace*—as opposed to supplement or augment—hard data with observations and other forms of analysis, the power of which is so restricted.

To gain some perspective, I searched for rationales that might serve to undermine a method that had served mankind so effectively and in so many other venues. I learned that the attacks on the science and on the evaluation tools on which scientific studies are based take on many forms, some of which overlap with one another. However, they tend to fall into two general categories. One is the idea that experimental research in the social sciences is just too difficult to carry out because it defies one's ability to maintain the degree of control necessary to make legitimate claims. The other source of dissatisfaction with the code-based evidence is its reliance on quantitative analysis, a method constructivists contend fails to consider the unique characteristics of individuals. Let's investigate these arguments.

Experimental Science in Reading—Yes We Can't

Some challenge the viability of investigative science in the social sciences, maintaining that human behavior—including that of children in classroom settings—is far too complex to lend itself to such devices. The justification for this claim is that such research is too "soft and squishy" because the behavior of individuals in groups is erratic and unpredictable and, thus, defies an experimenter's ability to prevent such factors from influencing test subjects. One proponent of this school of thought draws a distinction between the "easy-to-do" and the "hard-to-do" sciences:

> Easy-to-do science is what those in physics, chemistry, geology, and some other fields do. Hard-to-do science is what the social scientists do and, in particular, it is what we educational researchers do. In my estimation, we have the hardest-to-do science of them all![1]

According to this theorist, three major factors combine to make experimentation in the social sciences the hardest science of all: the power of contexts, the ubiquity of interactions, and the decade-by-decade findings. The contention is that researchers in the "hard-to-do" sciences cannot control for the countless variations that occur within testing groups. Matters like physical health, domestic abuse, test anxiety, or neighborhood violence can vary from day-to-day, and even minute-to-minute, thereby preventing the researcher from knowing their impact on students' ability to absorb a "treatment" and/or demonstrate achievement based on it.

The same can be said for the thousands of different ways students interact with their teachers and each other, most of which cannot be predicted or controlled. And, according to this school of thought, even if one could remove varying contexts and interactions as mitigating factors, the fluid nature of social attitudes and cultural norms are likely to render the findings from one decade irrelevant in the next.

The response from this author/practitioner (as opposed to an academic) to the notion that reading science is the "hardest of all" was to wonder why anyone would spend time making such a case. This is not how problems get solved or how society advances. I would maintain that teachers have the hardest job of all. But none of those with whom I worked ever wrote off a kid on that basis, much less thought to compose an essay about how hard his or her job may have been. It's like taking a position counter to the Obama campaign slogan and declaring, "Yes we can't."

My experience has been that those who spend their time talking about the difficulty of a task usually have one purpose in mind—to absolve themselves of responsibility for completing it. The truth of the matter is, while reading science does pose some very significant challenges, it is certainly not impossible to do. In fact, experimental scientists know quite well about such complexities and how their effects can be neutralized.

Yes, participants in a group will experience things that affect their performance. There will always be those suffering some long- or short-term illness, those who have test anxiety, or those who are in the middle of some family crisis—to name just a few extenuating circumstances. But, even though these are issues that merit our attention, there is absolutely no reason for them to waylay an experiment.

Built into the scientific method are powerful tools to ameliorate the impact of these conditions. Perhaps most compelling is something called *random assignment*. Random assignment, to both experimental (treatment) and control groups, ensures that any differences that occur because of varying interactions and contexts will be due to chance. Factors such as those described earlier will be evenly distributed among all groups, thereby canceling them out in the same way that like quantities can be removed from both sides of an algebraic equation. Those with test anxiety are as likely to be present in the testing group as the control group, thereby preventing that element from skewing the results.

Another way the scientific method resolves such issues is through sample size. The larger the sample size, the more a group tends to represent the general population. That is why the major reports I described earlier chose not to rely on any one study but instead based their conclusions on research syntheses, compilations of many studies whose aggregate sample size was exponentially larger than could be achieved from any single experiment. While it cannot remove these factors entirely, such a large sample size can significantly diminish their role in the findings and contribute mightily to revealing what a prosecutor might describe as a preponderance of the evidence. It is one thing for one study to validate a treatment; it is quite another when cumulative data from hundreds find essentially the same thing.

And in regard to the decade-by-decade argument (that a study completed in one decade is likely to be irrelevant in the next), consider the empirical evidence cited in chapter 4 that spanned over fifty years. Research synthesis after research synthesis continued to generate new data based on ever-more-refined research capabilities and yet the message remained essentially the same. The composite results reflected the findings of thousands of studies by distinguished scientists and winnowed from tens of thousands of others for their exemplary adherence to scientific protocols. What good does it do to invoke the decade-by-decade argument when the decade-by-decade results are always the same? How many decades will it take for someone to realize finally that, if we are looking to identify true obstacles to literacy, talking about how difficult it is to make such identification surely is one?

The "hard-to-do" argument is hard to fathom in other contexts also. First, I wonder if a research physicist looking at, for example, something like plasmon coupling in spherical multilayer nanoresonators would agree that such work fell into the "easy" category. And, second, would other social scientists accept the notion that they were incapable of isolating powerful effects through experimental designs? As one researcher put it:

> Admittedly, there are factors that make research in the social sciences more difficult, but it doesn't mean that we can't study human behavior in predictable ways. To suggest otherwise is to write off entire academic disciplines that study human behavior such as sociology, political science, economics, anthropology, and the like. Just ask scholars from those areas. The first thing they will tell you is that all human behavior is contextual, all human behavior is temporal, and all human behavior is interactive. And the second thing they will tell you is that research, when done correctly, can explain outcomes in predictable and generalizable ways.[2]

Dr. Jeff Lucas, professor of sociology at the University of Maryland, contends that investigative science is just as appropriate in reading as anywhere else, regardless of the complexities that accompany human behavior:

> I think the case could be made even stronger here for the advantage of an experimental approach. Conditions such as socioeconomic status, test anxiety, domestic violence, etc., that affect how kids perform in school do indeed make it difficult to isolate the effect of a given treatment. And that is why, if an experimenter can establish a positive link between a particular strategy and actual achievement in spite of all those extraneous factors, we should be especially confident in those results.[3]

Experimental Science in Reading—Does Not Treat Children as Individuals

Some also reject the scientific findings that support phonics for the same reason they object to phonics itself. Phonic methods, they maintain, are taught in a top-down, teacher-directed fashion that minimizes creativity and treats children as though they were all the same. The research studies that support phonics, according to these theorists, are guilty of the same transgression because they treat individual children as nothing more than data points to be subjected to cold and impersonal statistical analysis. A far more appropriate way to identify best practices, they maintain, is primarily through observational methods.

There is certainly much to be gained through observation, and in no way is it my intent to attack or delegitimize it. In fact, I would maintain that it is the best way to gain deep knowledge that can be used to address individual needs under specified circumstances. The problem occurs when one tries to generalize from one or a very small number of individual cases.

But even that information can be somewhat limiting, since looking at how individual students respond to a given treatment prevents us from observing whether another strategy would have served him or her to a greater or lesser extent. A researcher who notes that a particular student's reading improved, for example, with systematic phonics, cannot legitimately claim that it would not have improved as much or more with an alternative approach.

Conversely, research designs that compare randomly selected test subjects allow a researcher to make accurate predictions about the likelihood that a given effect will or will not work across a broad spectrum. Those who claim that such practices do not treat students like individuals are absolutely right. They cannot speak to any given individual, just as observational techniques lack the power to make broad assumptions about many.

Taking all this into account, it makes about as much sense to claim that one research platform is superior to the other as it does for adults to argue along the shore about whether swimming or use of a canoe would best facilitate the rescue of a drowning child. It is a matter of what is more appropriate in a given circumstance.

As a case in point, police in Minneapolis in the early 1980s needed to know the best way to prevent spousal abuse from recurring after responding to domestic violence calls. At the time, they had the options of arresting the perpetrator, ordering that person to leave the home, or providing on-site counseling. Lawrence Sherman and Richard Berk designed an experiment to identify which approach worked best. Before arriving at a home, police randomly decided which of the three approaches to follow. The researchers then tracked the suspects for the following six months.

The study found a significantly greater deterrence effect for arresting the suspects than for counseling or forced separation.[4] And they noted, "As a result of the experiment's findings, the Minneapolis Police Department changed its policy on domestic assault in early March of 1984," requiring officers "to file a written report explaining why they failed to make an arrest when it was legally possible to do so."[5] It is not surprising, therefore, that mandatory arrest became common practice in many communities and fifteen states passed legislation requiring that officers make arrests under such circumstances.[6]

The important point in this context is that Sherman and Berk's study did not treat people as individuals nor did they consider all the complicated things that contribute to domestic violence. Instead, it identified which approach worked best, on average, to reduce incidents of domestic violence. Arrest may or may not have been the best route to follow for any particular incident but, all other things being equal, those arrested were less likely to commit future assaults than those counseled or separated.

Spousal abuse is a significant public health concern that warrants serious and immediate attention, and society has a right to demand that law enforcement respond in a way that will protect its victims from further mistreatment. A lifetime of illiteracy poses a risk on a par with physical abuse (see chapters 11 and 12), and, therefore, it is hard to fathom that educators would not choose to base their actions on the same kind of verifiable data as that used by Sherman and Berk. Police must be held accountable for protecting citizens from harm. The educational community must be held equally accountable for the reading futures of its children.

Procrustean Beds

To the detriment of many children—most notably, those most at risk—some of the aforementioned gurus are unable or unwilling to acknowledge the kind of scientific principles cited above. Instead, they spin the matter in ways that sound plausible but have little basis in scientific fact. Consider the following statements from one of the most revered constructivist thinkers:

> Research that looks for general laws squeezes or stretches everyone to fit into Procrustean Beds. . . . Experimental research wants to treat everyone as the same; educational practice should always regard everyone as individuals.[7]

Those statements sound so self-evident, so humane, and so utterly respectful of individual children, even to those of us with limited knowledge of Procrustean beds. But after taking a little time to ponder the words, I could not help but view them as the kind of straw-man argument often seen in political ads. I won't even dwell on the fact that the writer is comparing two completely different constructs—educational *research* and educational *practice*—a rhetorical sleight of hand that essentially compares apples to oranges. But criticizing experimental science because it treats all kids the same is the same thing as criticizing experimental science for adhering to the rules of experimental science. It is analogous to criticizing the pope for promoting Catholicism.

Of course each individual is unique; no social scientist would ever claim otherwise. But the fact that *individuals* are diverse does not mean that scientific inquiry cannot draw accurate and, in many cases, generalizable conclusions about *group* outcomes. Assessing the efficacy of one reading method over another attempts to do exactly that: to determine whether students exposed to one technique, *on average*, do better than those who were not exposed to that technique. This has nothing to do with the unique traits of each child or each individual outcome; it has everything to do with which techniques work best for the largest number of students.

I have nothing but the highest regard for those who make passionate appeals for respecting the uniqueness of individual children. However, such appeals should never be used as a substitute for legitimately obtained evidence. Those who would have us do so appear to act with extreme hubris, writing off decades of authentic data with a dismissive wave of the hand and leaving vulnerable children to deal with the consequences.

STRATEGY #2: POLITICIZE THE SCIENCE

Another perspective found in the literature is that extreme conservatism is responsible for the phonics-based recommendations. Over the years, distinguished scientists who have found in favor of code-based instruction have been accused of such things as engaging in paradigm politics and of being "in bed with the far right." Driving this viewpoint is the notion that code-based proponents are pawns in a right-wing plot to attack public education and ingratiate American business as it attempts to privatize schools. In that same vein, some would have us view the experimental studies as perfidious machinations of religious fundamentalists who are trying to advance the cause of Bible study.

As previously stated, true science has no political agenda. And so, to anyone who charges that the far right is behind the initiative to promote code-based reading and attack constructivist principles, my response would be, "So what?"

What difference does it make if a Democrat or Republican, a Protestant or Catholic, a Sunni or a Shiite, chooses to advocate for or practice any particular type of reading instruction? That issue is irrelevant. The only question one needs to ask is, "Does it work?" Does it make any sense whatsoever to disregard valid scientific evidence on the basis of party affiliation or religious preference? It's neither politics nor religion that is at stake here. It's children and their futures.

Excerpt from
"We're failing our kids: No Child Left Behind has plenty of flaws, but throwing it out because it's a Republican plan is morally disgusting."
By Garrison Keillor
January 30, 2008
© Tribune Media Services, Inc.
All Rights Reserved. Reprinted with permission.

And then there is the grief that old righteous people inflict on the young, such as our public schools. I'm looking at U.S. Department of Education statistics on reading achievement and see that here in Minnesota—proud, progressive Minnesota—on a 500-point test (average score: 225), 27 percent of fourth-graders score below basic proficiency, and black and Hispanic kids score 30-some points lower than white on average, and the 30 percent of public school kids who come from households in poverty (who qualify for reduced-price school lunches) score 27 points lower than those who don't come from poverty.

Reading is the key to everything. Teaching children to read is a fundamental moral obligation of the society. That 27 percent are at serious risk of crippling illiteracy is an outrageous scandal.

This is a bleak picture for an old Democrat. Face it, the schools are not run by Republican oligarchs in top hats and spats but by perfectly nice, caring, sharing people, with a smattering of yoga/raga/tofu/mojo/mantra folks like my old confreres. Nice people are failing these kids, but when they are called on it, they get very huffy. When the grand poobah Ph.D.s of education stand up and blow, they speak with great confidence about theories of teaching, and considering the test results, the bums ought to be thrown out.

There is much evidence that teaching phonics really works, especially with kids with learning disabilities, a growing constituency. But because phonics is associated with behaviorism and with conservatives, and because the Current Occupant has spoken on the subject, my fellow liberals are opposed.

Liberal dogma says that each child is inherently gifted and will read if only he is read to. This was true of my grandson; it is demonstrably not true of many kids, including my sandy-haired, gap-toothed daughter. The No Child Left Behind initiative has plenty of flaws, but the Democrats who are trashing it should take another look at the Reading First program. It is morally disgusting if Democrats throw out Republican programs that are good for children. Life is not a scrimmage. Grown-ups who stick with dogma even though it condemns children to second-class lives should be put on buses and sent to North Dakota to hoe wheat for a year.

St. Michael, I beg you to send angels to watch over fourth-graders who are struggling to read because the righteous among us are not doing the job.

STRATEGY #3: OMIT THE SCIENCE

Until I began writing this book, my knowledge of reading science was superficial at best. If I had had a keener understanding of the code-based findings, I would have attempted to incorporate them into my lessons as a teacher. I would have done so in spite of the fact that I would have had few, if any, resources to assist me in delivering phonics training in the manner recommended by the data. I would have done so even at the risk of being characterized as someone who worked in opposition to the spirit of child-centrism or perhaps branded as some sort of drill-based lunatic.

But none of the training I received ever even mentioned the science or asked me to delve into it. This is true even though I earned licenses that qualified me to work as an elementary teacher, as a reading specialist for grades 1–12, as a high school teacher of English, and as an elementary school administrator. In one respect, it is mind-boggling to think I was so ill-informed and denied information so vital to the practice of my craft. But, in another, it should hardly have come as a surprise, given what I came to learn about the educational community's aversion to the scientific recommendations. In fact, we seem to have gone out of our way to adopt programs that worked aggressively to thwart a good share of its endorsements.

In the early 1990s, Art Levine noted in an article entitled "The Great Debate Revisited," that whole-language was the cause célèbre among teacher preparation institutions:

> Its influence is so pervasive that in 1987 a survey of forty-three texts used to train teachers of reading found that none advocated systematic phonics instruction—and only nine even mentioned that there was a debate on the issue.[8]

Those who would surmise that things are different today are simply wrong. As noted earlier in the National Council on Teacher Quality report (see page 18), reading research is conspicuous by its absence from reading-methods courses. In the twenty years that had elapsed since the survey referred to by Levine, three additional research syntheses replicated findings going back to the 1960s. Achievement gaps continued to expand, and government was attempting to impose strictures on schools that failed to show adequate progress. But none of those conditions seemed to alarm those whose responsibility it was to prepare teachers for careers in classrooms. For them, it remained business as usual, and they continued to pay little more than lip service to an ever-widening knowledge base that impacted directly on kids' reading development.

STRATEGY #4: REFUSE TO COMPROMISE

In my review of the literature, I found examples in which those affiliated with producing the major reports sought to extend the hand of compromise by advocating for holistic practices in a phonics-based environment. Following are two such examples:

> Whole-Language practices have come to predominate in regular classroom instruction in reading today for some good reasons. For example, the emphases on meaning, comprehension, writing, and the general philosophy of

integrating reading and writing to enhance meaning have had positive influences on literacy instruction. Research evaluating Whole-Language practices show that some children, who otherwise might not see a reason to read, learn to enjoy reading and writing when provided with these types of programs. The Whole-Language movement has increased the quality of literature in schools, provided more emphasis on library resources, and shifted the goal of reading instruction toward meaningfulness and enjoyment. Children and their families are encouraged to spend more time reading and writing, which clearly facilitates improved ability and interest. Positive attitudes toward reading are associated with Whole-Language practices.[9]

If, in fact, these are goals that drive the Whole-Language movement, then they must be supported whole-heartedly by all concerned. These goals are of paramount importance to our nation's health and progress. At the same time, however, they are strictly independent of the issues of the nature of the knowledge and processes involved in reading and learning to read. On these issues, the research is resoundingly clear. Only by disentangling these two key sets of issues can we give either the attention that each so urgently deserves.[10]

But strict constructivists were ill-inclined to accept such olive branches. The response of one was to gloat over the fact that research-based measures had failed to penetrate classroom practice to any discernible degree and that teachers continued to find whole-language methods more appealing. His words are both crass and smug:

It must have been terribly frustrating for these "scientists" to see the widespread enthusiasm among teachers for whole-language and the overt rejection of what they regarded as proven truth.[11]

And later,

[Teachers] actively reject the scientific word recognition paradigm as well as simplistic phonics programs because they have tested their knowledge base with their pupils in their classrooms and confirmed the validity of whole-language, not because they have been deprived of access to scientific knowledge.[12]

The writer may indeed be right that teachers prefer holistic methods; my experience would certainly attest to that. But in my mind, a response such as that comes across as sarcastic and juvenile. (Ha-ha, "scientists"! We win!) But might teachers—especially those who must meet the most challenging of needs—be willing to sacrifice their personal preferences if, by doing so, they could boast that all their kids were on level by the time they sent them on to the next grade? Might this be especially true with the ever-increasing pressure on them to raise achievement levels? Might these teachers be more than a little annoyed to learn that their professional training lacked some key elements? And how might they react upon discovering that systematic phonics strategies could have been incorporated into their practice in a way that didn't require them to sell their holistic and child-centric souls to the devil?

Some might contend that perhaps these theorists were demonstrating courage by refusing to compromise on principles that had guided them for so long. But how does one justify using methods unsupported by authentic science simply because it is what one holds near and dear to one's heart? That is reminiscent of the Catholic Church's actions in the 1600s when it put Galileo under house arrest for supporting the Copernican theory that the earth moved around the sun. Ultimately, the evidence became so compelling that the Church eventually capitulated and apologized to Galileo's heirs in 1992. *But it took three hundred and fifty years.* Is that how long our children will be made to wait for evidence-based instruction?

NOTES

1. Berliner, "Educational Research: The Hardest Science of All," *Educational Researcher*, November 2002, www.aera.net/pubs/er/toc/er3108.htm.
2. Dr. Teri Fritsma (sociologist specializing in research methodology and social stratification and senior project consultant, Minnesota State Colleges and University System), interview by author, November 11, 2008.
3. Lucas, telephone conference, July 22, 2008.
4. Sherman and Berk, "The Specific Deterrent Effects of Arrest for Domestic Assault," 261.
5. Sherman and Berk, "The Minneapolis Domestic Violence Experiment," 8.
6. Zorza, "The Criminal Law of Misdemeanor Domestic Violence," 1970–1990, 62.
7. Smith, *Unspeakable Acts, Unnatural Practices*, 36.
8. Levine, "The Great Debate Revisited," www.theatlantic.com/politics/education/levine.htm.
9. Pressley and Rankin, cited in Fletcher and Lyon, "Reading: A Research-Based Approach," 68.
10. Adams and Bruck, "Resolving the Great Debate," 18.
11. Goodman, "Who's Afraid of Whole-Language?," 15.
12. Goodman, "Who's Afraid of Whole-Language?," 3.

6

⤨

The Weak Arm of the Law

"Men are strong only so long as they represent a strong idea. They become powerless when they oppose it."

—Sigmund Freud

Before we continue, let's review what's happened up until this point. For eons, phonics reigns supreme because it never occurs to anyone that it would be wise to *withhold alphabetic training from those attempting to learn an alphabetic language.*

Nevertheless, progressive reformers conclude that it is more advantageous for children to learn whole words so as to spare them the drudgery of committing alphabetic patterns to memory. For learning purposes, this treatment essentially transforms an alphabetic language into a pictographic one. Over time, this new dynamic—often referred to as "whole-word" or "look-say"—gains a foothold and then dominates classroom practice for decades. Even so, some continue to oppose these progressive notions, and the two sides scratch and claw at one another, both asserting the superiority of their respective approaches.

To end the rancorous debate, experimenters begin subjecting the various methodologies to scientific inquiry, the assumption being that reading practitioners would adopt whatever the science validated. A fifty-year span of empirical data ensues, data that consistently indicate that phonic knowledge is an essential tool for achieving literacy, while also acknowledging that such alphabetic practices have no value unless they are used to facilitate fluency and comprehension. Some schools begin to implement programs that reflect the data and show remarkable results.

Government begins to take notice and the Department of Education launches an effort to promote research-based practices.

Despite the duality of the findings—that both phonics and meaning-based strategies are necessary to build early literacy—progressives nevertheless continue to rebuff the data, evidently finding it impossible to abide the presence of any form of direct and systematic anything and certainly the part-to-whole dynamic of code-based training. They continue to pursue their strictly holistic agenda and the reading wars continue unabated.

Throughout this painstaking saga, we can see several points at which cooler minds might have found a way to avert the bloodletting. For example, it might have been different if early educators had avoided the use of heavy-handed tactics to browbeat alphabetic drills into their cowering charges. But they didn't. Or perhaps history would have played out differently if Horace Mann had been less confrontational and mean-spirited toward the very people on whose shoulders it would rest to carry out his progressive reforms. But he wasn't.

Failing that, perhaps progressives might have been more vigilant in ascertaining the impact of their methods on achievement levels or, at least, been willing to entertain the notion that phonics and meaning-based approaches augmented, rather than defeated, one another. But they gave only cursory attention to that hypothesis. Maybe Rudolph Flesch could have softened his rhetoric and been more judicious in his denunciations of those he opposed. But it wasn't in his nature to do so.

And finally, in the wake of a burgeoning compilation of pure and applied data that authenticated the duality of the competing paradigms, perhaps those looking to put children first might somehow have found a way to integrate the two constructs. Perhaps rational thinkers, in the context of stagnating proficiency levels and ever-widening achievement gaps, might have confronted the reality of the collateral damage they continued to wreak upon those most vulnerable to reading failure. But such a phenomenon was not forthcoming. In fact, as it turned out, pretty much the opposite occurred.

FIGHTING FOR JOHNNY

We certainly had enough people willing to go out on a limb for Johnny. High-minded expressions of *children first*, *reading first*, and *all children can learn* abounded among schools and districts throughout the country and resonated in all the literature. But it was hardly a cohesive effort. A lot of energy was being expended, but whether or not it was on Johnny's behalf remained somewhat murky as ideologues continued to thumb their collective noses at the code-based recommendations of the scientific community.

There is something almost Orwellian about the situation. One faction manages to maintain primacy by engaging in a continuous campaign of misinformation and plausible deniability. They ignore the data, obfuscate its message, and make unwarranted claims in opposition to it. These claims have little basis in scientific fact, but they are so ubiquitous in the literature, and are so appealing to adult sensibilities, that few are willing to take issue with them.

BEST-LAID PLANS

It's not like we haven't tried to bridge this pedagogical chasm. Among the goals of the Reading Excellence Act (REA), signed into law by President Clinton in 1998, were to "teach every child to read by the end of third grade" and "improve the instructional practices of teachers and other instructional staff in elementary schools."[1]

The REA surmised that, if students were underperforming, chances are it was because the methods used to teach them were at odds with the scientific recommendations. The National Research Council's publication, *Preventing Reading Difficulties in Young Children*, noted this discrepancy. Citing a study by Deborah Simmons[2] et al. that examined the most popular basal reading programs, the authors report the following, among other findings:

- Phonological awareness activities occur, but in limited quantity and scope.
- The phonological awareness activities of segmenting and blending that are most highly correlated with beginning reading acquisition are simply *not* included in any of the basal reading programs.[3]

Even though I had been involved in public education for over thirty years when that report was released, I had no recollection of any staff development opportunity that addressed the so-called "best research and practice." As I indicated earlier, not only was such training unavailable, I encountered resistance when I sought to provide it on my own. Apparently school districts took full advantage of the fact that the REA included little, if any, ability to monitor program fidelity. Districts wrote grants that reflected what the Feds were looking for. Once the money was disbursed, schools simply used it to underwrite the cost of whatever it was they were doing in the past—programs that had failed Johnny for years.

The No Child Left Behind Act (NCLB) three years later tried to remedy that situation by establishing strict guidelines and subsidizing the cost of governmental oversight. But the matter was immediately politicized and mired in controversy. The reading community is remarkable in the dedication it manifests on behalf of children. However, it can be just as dedicated toward rebuffing any attempt to be held accountable for the practices it recommends. Among the charges leveled against the legislation are that it's punitive, relies too much on testing, is underfunded, is a sellout to right-wing fundamentalist causes, and represents heavy-handed intrusion of government into the autonomy of local districts. Any or none of those might be true, and, if I were guided strictly by my personal politics, I would likely be among those leading the charge against it. Indeed, NCLB has become such a political flash point that I run the risk of alienating many simply by bringing it up.

READING CONSPIRACY

But it's not really NCLB that I choose to defend. Rather, it is the fundamental principle upon which it is based—the use of scientifically validated programs, especially for those most vulnerable to reading failure. So it matters little to me which program can succeed in bringing that about, just as it is of little import whether a Republican or Democratic administration launches it or whether a Christian conservative or Orthodox Jew supports it.

None of those things matter if Johnny learns to read.

Evidently, however, that is not how others choose to frame the issue since we have shown ourselves to be incapable of preventing our personal ideologies from impacting on the stated goal. Since NCLB advocated for research-based methods and was launched by a Republican administration, the very term "research-based" became a code word for conservative and fundamentalist principles and something to be scorned and vilified by more liberal thinkers. That is an interesting phenomenon since we liberals seem to embrace science when it comes to such things as global warming and evolutionary theory. I will not get into those matters other than to say it's a good thing Edward Jenner was not a Communist or we might still be facing massive outbreaks of smallpox.

UNSPEAKABLE PRACTICES, UNNATURAL ACTS

No Child Left Behind thereby represented a new front in the struggle for instructional dominance. Anti-reading-science-based factions went on the offensive and devised strategies to undermine those premises upon which NCLB was based. One highly regarded author referred to the scientific narrative as "the Just So story—Just S-O—Just Sound Out, and you can read."[4] His article promoting this point of view, first published as "The

Just So Story—Obvious But False" in *Language Arts*,[5] was later included as a chapter in his collection of anti-phonics essays entitled *Unspeakable Acts, Unnatural Practices: Flaws and Fallacies in "Scientific" Reading Instruction.*

The book's back cover states: "The mandated approach to language teaching is, in fact, linguistically impossible, as the author proves." I looked for such proof but could find no corroboration in the book for any of the claims. And so I dug through the stacks at the library until I found the volume of *Language Arts* that contained the issue in which the article originally appeared. Amazingly, it contained not one footnote, nor a bibliography, nor a list of references. Nothing. Even so, the book was warmly received and appeared on lists of recommended readings for teachers in training. The following is taken from a review:

> Smith reduces our educational problems to a simple dichotomy. You either believe that learning occurs naturally or unnaturally. If you believe that learning is unnatural than [sic] all sort [sic] of mechanistic systems must be devised to ensure that a person learns, even if the learner has other impulses.
>
> This profound new book makes a great read and a fabulous holiday gift for your staff, friends, or relatives interested in creating the most productive learning experiences possible for children.[6]

Still, NCLB was not about to go away and holistic writers and theorists realized they would need to find ways for schools to show that they were deferring to scientifically based reading research (SBRR) practices. They developed a program called "Balanced Literacy" to make it appear as though they were embracing scientifically validated practices. "Balanced Literacy" turned out to be essentially the same holistic programs containing some incidental and superficial code-based treatment, so as to dodge the appearance of phonic impropriety.

DUBIOUS SCIENCE

Another means to undermine the scientific findings was to engage in questionable research practices and then attempt to pass them off as reliable data. One such study used a $340,000 grant from the state of Wisconsin to conduct a three-year longitudinal analysis of direct instruction (DI). As luck would have it, the investigation found that DI was less effective than what was offered through traditional basal programs that stressed holistic practices. Among its findings:

- Students in first, second, and third grade receiving Direct Instruction scored significantly lower on their overall reading achievement than students receiving more traditional forms of reading instruction. These results were consistent in urban and suburban schools.

- Students in first, second, and third grade receiving Direct Instruction scored significant[ly] lower on measures of comprehension than students receiving more traditional forms of reading instruction.
- First graders in an urban school district receiving Direct Instruction scored significantly lower on decoding and comprehension than students receiving more traditional forms of reading instruction.
- These results were consistent across three consecutive school years.
- Overall, on measures of reading achievement, students receiving more traditional forms of reading instruction in urban and suburban school districts display significantly greater gains than students receiving Direct Instruction.[7]

The report was widely circulated and appeared in a mainstream educational journal. Lost in all the hoopla surrounding the announcement was the fact that the experiment was a methodological disaster.

First, the author steered clear of test sites where DI had been most effective, meaning that a significant portion of the teachers delivering it had only marginal training in its use. But that was just the beginning. The study could not maintain a sample size large enough to demonstrate statistical power nor was it able to sustain parallel groupings. But perhaps worst of all, it had no business labeling itself as longitudinal. Longitudinal studies are supposed to track the progress of the same individuals over time. However, when the three-year project was completed, few children from the first year were around to be tested. Calling it a longitudinal study was essentially a contradiction in terms.

The What Works Clearinghouse (WWC), a division of the U.S. Department of Education's Institute of Education Studies, included the experiment among a group that "does not meet WWC evidence standards because the intervention and comparison groups are not shown to be equivalent at baseline."[8]

A detailed analysis of the study was conducted by Gary Adams, an education professor at George Fox University, Portland, Oregon. Adams decided to use the experiment as a class project for his EDFL 701 Research Seminar. He and his team of graduate students found multiple methodological errors, including the use of inappropriate statistical analysis, and the above-mentioned issues of sample size, parallel groupings, and calling it a longitudinal study.

Adams and his team recommended the following:

Assuming that Year 1 of a three-year $340,000 grant must have cost approximately $100,000, the best thing would have been to start over. There is no way that a longitudinal study should have been attempted with such small sample sizes. At this point, the author was throwing money away on a doomed project.[9]

At the end of the second year, Adams's group advised:

At a cost of probably around $200,000 and two years of effort, the investigator should have probably stopped this study because there were only three students remaining from the original group and thus, no longer qualified as longitudinal.[10]

Why, the group wondered, would he continue with it and issue a report that was so misleading?

One could only speculate as to how an advisor to a doctoral candidate would have viewed such an amateurish attempt at quantitative analysis. Nevertheless, despite such egregious methodological shortcomings and despite the fact that it was never subjected to peer review, a major educational journal published it under the headline "Study Challenges Direct Reading Method."[11]

As a result, an oft-validated program gets ambushed by invalidly derived data, and many in the reading community applaud the effort and circulate the results far and wide. Not only are children the victims, but so are teachers looking to upgrade their ability to build effective readers by taking the time to delve into the professional literature. Those reading the article would conclude in good faith that DI was something to avoid even though the experiment did little, if anything, to make such a case.

SHOW ME THE MONEY

As stated earlier, opponents of NCLB characterized it as an unfunded mandate. That is an easy charge to level at any kind of legislation that has a fiscal impact on local budgets, and I was among the first to castigate it for that reason. However, deeper inspection caused me to view it in a different light. The federal government subsidizes schools mainly through Title I, but such funds represent but a small fraction of what it takes to educate children. State and district funding sources far outweigh what the federal government can provide. Through NCLB, the Department of Education was simply attempting to steer states and districts toward use of programs with a proven track record. So it really wasn't a matter of calling for extra spending; it was more about using the money that was available to the best possible advantage. The message was essentially, "Don't spend more; spend more wisely," something akin to the superintendent's message, "Don't work longer; work smarter."

READING FIRST

The government sought to be a model in that respect through a program known as Reading First. Not only would it address the criticism related to funding, it would also show states and districts how to put its money for reading education to best use, especially in a climate of ever-shrinking resources. Reading First set aside over $1 billion for schools and districts to improve the reading performance of students during a critical period for literacy development—kindergarten through third grade. The money was also designed to help those who already had established reading deficits and those living below poverty levels.

Reading First allocated the money to the states which were then responsible for reviewing grant applications and monitoring compliance of those who qualified. The Feds were anxious to avoid what had happened in 1998 under the Reading Excellence Act when schools accepted dollars but often failed to use the money in the prescribed manner. Reading First not only represented a renewed effort to steer education dollars toward scientifically validated programs but also tried to go a step further than the REA by closing off escape routes from the NCLB's provisions. There was hope that, at long last, schools could claim, a la the Good Housekeeping Seal of Approval, that the methods used to teach children to read had met rigid standards for effectiveness. But it didn't happen that way.

There appeared to be cause for optimism at the onset. Several districts reported significant progress after having bought into the spirit of Reading First and implementing its requirements. The General Accounting Office (GAO) issued a report that stated, according to one writer on education reform:

> Reading First was making solid progress toward its objective of lifting the reading achievement of economically disadvantaged children. The GAO found (according to its executive summary) that "nearly seventy percent of states reported that reading instruction has improved greatly or very greatly since the implementation of Reading First." Furthermore, "Every state reported improvements in professional development because of Reading First and at least forty-one states reported that professional development improved greatly or very greatly in five key instructional areas."[12]

Suddenly it became apparent that this legislation had legs and the Feds were serious. Schools and book publishers might actually need to modify their approaches or risk being omitted from consideration for Reading First dollars.

But that didn't happen either. Many in education continued to balk at the "clinically proven" requirement, maintaining that their programs were as scientifically based as any. Textbook publishers, long dominated by constructivist pedagogy, started to lobby members of Congress. Their purpose was to get their programs approved as acceptable under Reading First even though there was little, if any, hard data to recommend them. Democratic members of Congress were more than happy to oblige, having heard numerous complaints from their constituents. Furthermore, they were happy to undermine the efforts of an administration that had thwarted its legislation at every turn. It was a great chance for political payback.

Next, there were complaints that the NCLB was too restrictive and might possibly be in violation of the provisions of a Department of Education law that prohibited it from imposing specified measures on school districts. Ironically, this law had been a Republican effort to lessen governmental interference in local matters. Now that same law was working to its detriment.

On that basis, the GAO faulted the program based on the following taken directly from its report:

> [The Department of] Education lacked an adequate set of controls to ensure that Reading First's requirements were followed, while at the same time ensuring that it did not intervene into state and local curricular decisions.[13]

This was fodder for a Joseph Heller novel. Consider the plight of Chris Doherty, Reading First's director, assigned the task of certifying that the intent of the program was properly administered. His stated mission was to assure that Reading First monies were apportioned based on the research criteria. If he approved those that did not meet the NCLB's requirements, he was failing in his responsibility to Reading First. If, on the other hand, he rejected untested approaches, then he was being program specific and in violation of the law. Under such circumstances, how does one act on behalf of one guideline without violating the other? If ever there were a catch-22, this was surely it.

Those opposed to the underlying principles of Reading First took full advantage and began engaging in a new round of attacks designed to weaken the law's provisions. They claimed that their chosen programs were as science-based as any other, that the director was biased, and that the NCLB could not deny them without infringing on the curricular decisions of individual states.

Eventually, Doherty was forced to cave in to a more expansive interpretation of the scientific benchmark. Schools only needed to show some sort of link to research-based practices and no longer needed to submit evidence based on clinical trials. The result was that many were able to qualify for Reading First grants while continuing to proceed much as they had in the past. Thus, Reading First reflected a wide swath of the pedagogical spectrum, a condition that essentially undermined the guiding principles upon which it was established. The reduced standards forced acceptance of programs that contained any kind of vague or oblique reference to elements prescribed by the data. Suddenly, all were contending that their programs for early literacy qualified them for inclusion under Reading First, and review teams were severely constrained in their ability to deny such claims.

The assertion by some that Doherty was biased was based on his previous association with DI. I can understand how that might lend at least the appearance of impropriety, but there are other factors to consider. First, who better to lead an initiative that was pushing for scientifically based programs than one who had spent his career doing that very thing and whose background lay in a program that pioneered research-based techniques? Second, no one ever accused Doherty of any type of quid pro quo deals that would line his pockets or otherwise advance his career. In fact, DI—perhaps the most scientifically validated of all programs—actually lost market share during the Reading First funding cycles, an indication that those who were attempting to undercut the movement toward validated practices were succeeding quite well.

Even so, Doherty still had some fight left in him, a character trait that proved to be his downfall. Despite the diluted norms for funding, he was still committed to upholding the spirit of Reading First. Matters were on a collision course, and, suddenly, we were right back to the same kind of heated rhetoric used by Horace Mann and Rudolph Flesch. Doherty had a meltdown when he learned that the Wright Group was attempting to cash in on Reading First. The Wright Group, with its Big Books and rigid adherence to constructivism, operated in diametric opposition to direct and systematic code-based practices and, in fact, had never even aspired to the scientific imprimatur (called SBRR, for Scientifically Based Reading Research). Mirroring the outrage so prevalent in the reading debates, Doherty, in an e-mail, directed his people to quash this holistic abomination of Reading First. Once he pressed "Send," he was history. According to one source, the e-mail read:

> Beat the s_ _ t out of them in a way that will stand up to any level of legal and [whole-language] apologist scrutiny. Hit them over and over with definitive evidence that they are not SBRR, never have been and never will be.[14]

THE PANGLOSS INDEX

The diminution of the standard for Reading First is but one example of the ingenious ways found to bypass standards, duck accountability, and keep Johnny from advancing in an age-appropriate fashion. A 2006 report by the Education Sector discovered an interesting phenomenon while attempting to rank states based on their compliance with standards set by NCLB. This ranking, which came to be known as the Pangloss Index, found a negative correlation between how schools complied with NCLB and how they actually achieved. Kevin Carey, Education Sector's research and policy manager, explained the dichotomy:

> On the whole, the index was less indicative of which states were actually doing well than which states had simply chosen to *define* themselves as doing well. Mediocre states made themselves out to be great and low-performing states snuck into the Top 10, while a number of objectively higher-performing states ranked near the bottom. . . . Thus, the list was dubbed "The Pangloss Index," after the character in Voltaire's *Candide* who insisted—in the face of all evidence to the contrary—that we live in the best of all possible worlds.[15]

Alabama, for example, had a Pangloss ranking of 5,[16] meaning that it ranked in the top 10 percent of states at meeting its achievement goals under NCLB. However, the National Assessment of Educational Progress reported that only 29 percent of Alabama's fourth graders could read at a proficient level, up slightly from the previous year, but a pretty dismal performance record all the same.[17] Compare that with fourth graders in Massachusetts who performed nearly 70 percent better in reading than those in Alabama,[18] yet whose Pangloss ranking was 46, or in the bottom 10 percent at meeting NCLB benchmarks.[19]

Alabama may not have shown much ability to build more and better readers, but it was exceptionally adroit at finding ways to lower the bar, creating standards of accountability vastly easier to attain than what had previously been the case. In fact, Alabama has been so remarkably successful at identifying this loophole that other states have seized the opportunity to emulate their practices. As Carey put it, "Collectively, these states and districts provide a case study in how determined states can undermine even tightly constructed laws like NCLB."[20]

In other words, our best attempts to establish high standards and gear schools toward effective practices have so far been a bust. In this regard, it is not Johnny who has failed. Rather, it is we who have failed Johnny, when our main focus is to circumvent requirements, sustain practices that continue to put Johnny at an ever-greater disadvantage, and duck accountability for what happens in the aftermath. If it is conflict of interest that we are all so concerned about, consider the conflict between what Johnny needs and what he actually gets. How, indeed, is that an expression of *children first*?

NOTES

1. U.S. Department of Education Archived Information, *The Reading Excellence Act*, www.ed.gov/inits/FY99/1-read.html.

2. Simmons et al., "Translating Research into Basal Reading Programs," 9–13.

3. Snow, Burns, and Griffin, eds., *Preventing Reading Difficulties in Young Children*, 192.

4. Smith, *Unspeakable Acts, Unnatural Practices*, 40.

5. *Language Arts* 80 (4): 256–58.

6. Stager, "Meet Frank Smith," www.thefreelibrary.com/Meet+Frank+Smith:+gifts+of+wisdom+for+educators.-a0111647619.

7. Ryder, Sekulski, and Silberg, "Results of Direct Instruction Reading Program Evaluation Longitudinal Results," 4.

8. What Works Clearinghouse, *Intervention: Reading Mastery*, August 2008, 3.

9. Adams, et al., "A Critical Review of Randall Ryder's Report of Direct Instruction Reading in Two Wisconsin School Districts."

10. Adams, et al., "A Critical Review."

11. Manzo, "Study Challenges Direct Reading Method," *Education Week*, January 28, 2004.

12. Stern, *Too Good to Last*, 32–33.

13. U.S. GAO, *Reading First*, 35.

14. Stern, *Too Good to Last*, 27.

15. Carey, *The Pangloss Index*, 4.

16. Carey, *The Pangloss Index*, 4.

17. Institute of Education Sciences, National Center for Education Statistics, *The Nation's Report Card: Reading 2007 State Snapshot Report*, Alabama.

18. Institute of Education Sciences, National Center for Education Statistics, *The Nation's Report Card: Reading 2007 State Snapshot Report*, Massachusetts.

19. Carey, *The Pangloss Index*, 4.

20. Carey, *The Pangloss Index*, 3.

7

~

So Shall We Reap

"Why don't we just stop everything when kids aren't learning to read? Why are we even doing anything else?"

—Dr. Alex Granzin, past president, Oregon School Psychologists Association

Previous chapters have described how one approach—combining mastery of the alphabetic code with the more popular programs for helping children achieve "whole-language" skills—embraces the research on early reading by employing direct, intensive, systematic, explicit, and comprehensive measures for the teaching of reading. I will be the first to admit that I cannot make a statistical argument that most schools do not operate in such a fashion but, given my experience and investigations into the matter, it is hard for me to conclude otherwise.

If the research is correct—that children stand to benefit from systematic alphabetic training—and we nevertheless refuse to provide it, then the onus for the inability of many children to read begins to rest more on our shoulders than on the shoulders of those who are thereby victimized. Consider the consequences of an institutionally orchestrated attempt to obstruct and stonewall a scientific message that may not have much appeal for adults but just might hold the key to Johnny's future. Do we ever really stop to consider how that affects not only Johnny but the rest of us as well? Making good on our promises to put children first requires that we confront some realities—some inconvenient truths, as Al Gore might put it.

INESTIMABLE COSTS

Individuals at the lowest literacy levels face bleak prospects. According to the National Institute for Literacy (NIFL), 43 percent live in poverty, 17 percent receive food stamps, and 70 percent have no full or part-time jobs.[1] That is a perilous condition in which to live, but we all pay a price. Robert Sweet has noted:

> More than half of Fortune 500 companies have become educators of last resort, with the cost of remedial employee training in the three Rs reaching more than 300 million dollars a year. One estimate places the yearly cost in welfare programs and unemployment compensation due to illiteracy at six billion dollars. An additional 237 billion dollars a year in unrealized earnings is forfeited by persons who lack basic reading skills, according to Literacy Volunteers of America.[2]

Illiteracy and low literacy prevent individuals from attaining higher levels of education and significantly increase the likelihood that they will, at some point, be imprisoned. The incarceration rate for white males with a high school diploma is about 0.3 percent, compared to 0.8 percent for high school dropouts. Among African-American males, the incarceration rate is over 3.5 percent for dropouts, as compared to 2 percent for those with diplomas.[3] Economist Enrico Moretti estimates the social benefit of increasing the graduation rate by a mere 1 percent at a staggering $1.7 billion.[4]

JOBS

Consider the impact on our economy when we cannot produce a work-force capable of addressing the increased demands of a society that must compete globally. Today, even low-paid individuals must perform tasks that were once done by those in managerial positions. For example, the guy in the auto parts store must be able to do things that never would have been required in the past, such as reading and comprehending technical service manuals, managing and tracking inventory, and writing reports in response to problems.

We have seen that many of these tasks can be outsourced to foreign nations when it becomes difficult to find competent individuals in our own country. I cannot help but wonder whether we will soon find someone in Malaysia, via video feed, doing everything from taking and processing orders at the McDonald's drive-through window to advising customers at Home Depot.

HEALTH CARE

As noted earlier, those with low or marginal literacy are more likely to be unemployed and, therefore, less likely to be covered by health insurance. They must rely on government assistance programs at an untold cost to taxpayers. But whether they have coverage or not, the cost grows exponentially when you consider that low-literacy individuals have a difficult time interpreting the literature that advises them on how to stay healthy or what actions to take when they do become sick or are injured. Their inability to comprehend written material causes them to seek medical attention at doctors' offices or hospital emergency rooms when there really is no need to do so. It has been estimated that nearly half of hospital visits are unnecessary and result from individuals being unable to grasp what is easily available in printed form.[5]

Low-literacy individuals can also experience difficulty taking advantage of free services that would assist them in managing illnesses so as to keep them from becoming emergencies. We were fortunate at my school to have an on-site clinic staffed by a nurse-practitioner (NP) who provided free services to our students, including the 92 percent who lived below poverty thresholds. The NP had both the skills and the authority to communicate with family doctors, write prescriptions, help kids manage their chronic asthma and diabetic conditions, administer immunizations, and provide numerous other services that helped keep our kids healthy and attending school regularly. But low literacy may well have kept many parents from availing themselves of these benefits. We often had a difficult time getting some to sign off on a form giving us permission to treat their children. They might well have been fearful that they were authorizing something they didn't want or didn't comprehend the need for.

LITERACY AND DEMOCRACY

Low literacy also has a direct impact on the effective functioning of democratic principles. The fact that elections have been reduced to a battle of sound bites is a testament to citizens' unwillingness or inability to sort through printed material and make judgments based on deep knowledge. To do these things requires sufficient reading fluency to take in multiple perspectives and to make sense of the complex interactions between people and events.

Even the act of voting itself requires the ability to read and follow procedures necessary to make a vote count. Recounts reveal just how incapable many are at interpreting what is necessary to assure that their votes will be properly recorded. Is it unreasonable to accept the notion that, in the 2000 presidential election, the loss of ballots in Florida could be attributed more to literacy problems than to faulty machines?

SOCIAL JUSTICE

There are few social ills the root causes of which don't have some connection to low or nonexistent reading ability. Prior to the invention of the alphabet, literacy in pictographic languages was a skill reserved strictly for privileged classes—a condition that kept the vast share of economic resources in the hands of a few and allowed those in royal positions to enslave and otherwise subjugate their fellow human beings.

Since the appearance of alphabetic (as opposed to pictographic) languages brought literacy ability to the common person, it was seen as one of the greatest exercises in democracy the world had ever experienced. This all began in the Mediterranean region around 1500 B.C. But exactly how much progress have we made over those eons of time? How, after some 3,500 years, can we explain the inability of so many to take advantage of this fundamental tool for literacy? How do we account for the fact that, while virtually everyone has the capability to learn these concepts, we have chosen not to teach them?

It is reminiscent of the days when literacy training of any kind was withheld from those victimized by America's experiment with slavery. We may have abolished that institution but lack of literacy ability keeps a large share of minorities firmly entrenched in a state of servitude. An article in the July 2008 issue of *Teacher Magazine* noted:

> In the 40 years since integration, the African-American achievement gap in education stubbornly persists even though other racial groups have arrived as immigrants, been assimilated, and demonstrated more educational progress. In terms of percentages, African-Americans far outweigh others in their representation in the prison population. Why is it that our fellow citizens continue to figure so largely on the statistical bottom rung of the socioeconomic ladder? If education is the way up and out of poverty and social stagnation, why have we continued to fail to bring this group to the table?[6]

After reading that passage, I couldn't help but recall the comment of a student who uttered, "Always trying to keep the black man down," when, for disciplinary reasons, his teacher confiscated his safety cadet belt. We all got a chuckle out of that. But the matter of keeping minorities oppressed is not funny, and, at some point, we must confront the reality that in many ways we have neglected many.

We have done so *not* by making students accountable for their behavior, or by denying them privileges, such as membership in the school's safety patrol. Rather, we have kept them down by denying them the instruction found to be of greatest benefit to them. When that is the case, it is hard to conclude anything other than that discrimination is alive and well in American society. We can claim it is about jobs and wages, but it is more about education levels, which ultimately lead to disparities in jobs and wages. Indeed, economic disparities disappear when you make comparisons based strictly on educational attainment. And yet we continue to rely on methods that serve upper and middle-class children just fine but which neglect those less fortunate. When such a condition is allowed to continue for so long, we demonstrate a failure of mission to provide a free and appropriate public education, not just to some, but to all. It is bigotry in its purest form and, for that, we must be held accountable.

SOCIAL ISOLATION

Low-literacy individuals must find ways to cope. Some tend to withdraw into a self-imposed state of isolation. They bypass elections and are unwilling to assert their rights as consumers or to question procedures at their children's schools. They have little faith that the system can ever work to their advantage and view outreach efforts with resentment and cynicism. In many cases, they find it preferable to retreat to the safety of a social cocoon where their main goal is simply to be left alone.

SOCIAL AGGRESSION

Others often take a different path, one of violence and aggression. These individuals realize their literacy shortcomings will ultimately deny them any legitimate means to participate in the American dream of prosperity, safety, and security. And so they engage in high-risk behaviors that often land them in the criminal justice system. Their experiences in the projects, on the streets, and in poverty compromise their freedom on a par with life in a jail cell and so the risks appear less formidable. They don't really see that they have all that much to lose since they have little hope of improving their situations.

Those who might take offense at the notion that low reading ability leads to a life of crime and imprisonment are merely burying their heads in the sand. Consider this excerpt of an interview between David Boulton and Dr. Grover (Russ) Whitehurst, director of the Institute of Education

Sciences, taken from *Children of the Code*, a series shown on public television, dealing with the current reading crisis:

Boulton:	We were interviewing Lesley Morrow, the past-president of the International Reading Association, and she made a statement which flabbergasted me. She said this was a fact: that there are some states that determine how many prison cells to build based on reading scores.
Whitehurst:	Yes. Again, the predictability of reading for life success is so strong that if you look at the proportion of middle-schoolers who are not at the basic level, who are really behind in reading, it is a very strong predictor of problems with the law and the need for jails down the line.

                                   Literacy for societies, literacy for states, literacy for individuals is a powerful determinant of success. The opposite of success is failure and, clearly, being in jail is a sign of failure.

                                   People who don't read well have trouble earning a living. It becomes attractive, in some cases the only alternative in terms of gaining funds, to violate the law and steal, to do things that get you in trouble. Few options in some cases other than to pursue that life. Of course reading opens doors.[7]

Another source buttresses that perspective:

Evidence shows that children who do not read by third grade often fail to catch up and are more likely to drop out of school, take drugs, or go to prison. So many nonreaders end up in jail that Arizona officials have found they can use the rate of illiteracy to help calculate future prison needs.[8]

None of this bodes well, given that over 80 percent of African-American, Hispanic, and Native American fourth-graders are less than proficient readers, while over half of those same individuals cannot read at even a basic level.[9] Those figures are like a death warrant for a significant share of our kids. Juvenile offenders are typically at a ninth or tenth-grade level but have the reading ability of a fourth-grader.[10] And what happens to these adjudicated youth once they are released? Only 12 percent manage to get a high school diploma or GED, 70 percent are neither in school nor employed a year after their release, and they are seven times more likely to be unemployed and on welfare as an adult.[11]

Interview with Pat Pawlak,
Education Director, Minnesota Correctional Facility-Stillwater

Pat Pawlak is the education director at a high-security state prison in Stillwater, Minnesota, the largest of nine facilities governed by the Minnesota Department of Corrections. She and her staff administer programs to inmates designed to build their literacy ability and to help them qualify for a high school GED and beyond.

Ms. Pawlak was kind enough to give me some of her time to inquire about the attributes of prisoners who must work to attain skills they should have mastered long ago.

Q. How would you describe those who are in your program?

A. There are a few exceptions, but otherwise they are as you would expect among a prison population. They are males who come from poor, one-parent families and who reside in inner-city environments where drugs, violence, and gangs tend to predominate.

Q. Still, not everyone who comes from such an environment winds up in a high-security prison. Are there other attributes you notice?

A. Yes. I have found that they have rarely enjoyed the kind of stability most of us take for granted. They may be with Mom for a time, then Grandma, Auntie, and, in many cases, foster care. We all need to experience a sense of belonging. If they can't get that through family, they will seek it elsewhere, such as in a gang.

   Also, education was not something that was valued in their lives, even when their parents claimed otherwise. Many fell behind early in school and, when they couldn't get any positive reinforcement, they would seek attention by engaging in negative behaviors.

Q. Are your methods different than those used in the schools?

A. We use whatever works best.

Q. Research shows that phonics ability is central to literacy attainment. Do you teach phonics to thirty, forty, and fifty-year-olds?

A. Yes, of course. If a student needs phonics training, he gets it. There is no shame in that. The goal is to make him a reader, not worry about what it might look like to others. Believe it or not, some can even be motivated with stickers. If that works, we will provide stickers.

Q. Would you say their attitude toward school is more positive now than it was prior to their incarceration?

A. Yes, I believe it is. Of course there are exceptions to the rule but, as a whole, we have few problems. Most work hard to gain admittance to our programs and conduct themselves in a way that will allow them to continue. They all want to finish, to accomplish something, to succeed where they had failed in the past. Nearly all of them make it—get their GED, that is.

Q. How is it that you can succeed where the schools have failed?

A. Well, I always say that we have to be better than the public schools because that is where they managed to fall between the cracks. But the schools have a tough job. It is not easy to teach kids who are hungry, suffering from posttraumatic stress disorder, and who might not know where they will be sleeping that night. It can become overwhelming. I had one inmate tell me that he once had a teacher who bribed him with candy to sit in the back of the room and simply be quiet.

Q. But don't you need to deal with those same problems to an even greater extent?

A. Maybe. But if inmates no longer have a desire to learn, you couldn't prove it by me. They have a desperate desire to succeed.

Q. Why would learning mean so much to them at this point, when it might be too late to take advantage of what, let's say, a GED might provide?

A. Well, first of all, they have come to realize that there is joy in just learning something, no matter what it is. And secondly, their need for a sense of self-worth is greater than at any time in their lives. It is something they have always lacked and they are more motivated than ever to gain that sense of esteem. We do our best to build upon that natural inclination.

But we make it clear to all our students that we cannot just give it out, that they must accept things that are difficult and succeed in spite of them. Nothing builds esteem more than accomplishment. Maybe if they had achieved more success early in their lives, they might not be with us now. But the fact remains that they are as motivated as anyone else to show the ability to achieve something meaningful, regardless of their current situation.

Q. Would you say that is always true? What about those who will die in your facility?

A. Many of them will die here. But it doesn't seem to matter. We have an inmate who will never get beyond these walls. When he arrived, I encouraged him to work toward his GED. He wondered why I would even suggest that, given he would never see the light of day. I said, if nothing else, it would sure make his family proud of him, to come and see him graduate. He told me that his family had long ago disowned him and no one would ever show up for such an event. But after awhile, he came around and asked to be admitted into the program. He was the featured speaker at his own graduation.

Q. What could the schools do to generate that same kind of motivation?

A. As I said earlier, I cannot judge the schools. Our situations are very different. But I do know from my experience that human beings have a natural inclination to succeed and that they know the difference between what is real and what is contrived. If we keep our expectations high and provide the kind of support that will allow them to make it, they will take full advantage of what we offer.*

*The preceding interview reflects the opinions of Ms. Pawlak and does not necessarily represent those of the Minnesota Department of Corrections.

SO WHAT ARE WE GOING TO DO ABOUT IT?

When it comes to staring down the literacy crisis our country now faces, we have been at a crossroads for some time. We have identified the problem, we are aware of its ramifications for individuals and for our future as a nation, and we cannot avoid the reality that conventional practices have left too many behind for far too long. It is time to ask, "What are we going to do now that is different? What will give us the greatest chance of moving forward?"

As a coach to other principals, I was taught to listen actively to my clients. I was to probe constantly for information as they articulated the challenges they faced, determined the conditions that may have caused them, and identified obstacles that lay in the path of their resolution. Ultimately, however, the question had to arise, "Now that you are aware of all the issues, what are you going to do about it? What steps will you take to address the circumstances and move on from there?"

Chapter 7

CHANGING PROFESSIONAL BEHAVIOR

It is one thing to develop an action plan and another to carry it out. Oftentimes, this requires a change in behavior, a migration from a comfort zone that serves us well for the moment but keeps us from venturing into unknown territory. It is a scary prospect but the only means of ascending to the next plateau.

Embarking on such a path will require some modification to the way we approach teaching and learning and a reexamination of what has been so sacrosanct in the past, things like reading readiness, developmental appropriateness, and curricular autonomy.

Pursuing research-based methods will also require standing up to those who would discourage any such notions. These individuals wield enormous power and influence and are willing to attack anyone and anything that poses a threat to their version of orthodoxy. Their influence is so pervasive and so unyielding that I once heard them referred to as the reading mafia. Anyone with the temerity to challenge their doctrinaire approaches might want to watch his or her back for fear that some nefarious force might be lurking nearby.

When discussing *Leaving Johnny Behind* with one reading scholar, he ended the conversation by saying that he admired my courage. I won't lie by claiming I didn't appreciate the comment. But why would the act of advocating for clinically proven methods be an act of courage? Is it a courageous act for a doctor to base his practice on verifiably effective treatments? Is it courageous for a structural engineer to recommend steel for a bridge with the tensile strength to protect those who ride atop it every day?

All this serves to illustrate just how anesthetized the reading community has become. Instead of moving forward with the knowledge at hand, it is content to engage in endless political, ideological, and philosophical discussions and to somehow make that look as though it were doing something meaningful to address the reading crisis. You can't blame a poor kid, or a minority kid, or a dyslexic kid, or an English as a Second Language learner for that. That negligence is entirely on us, the adults who are supposed to know better. As Johnny Cochran might have put it, "It's malicious, it's preposterous, it's egregious." But amazingly, it is true.

Dr. Martin Haberman, creator of the National Teacher Corps, noted:

> We create a city the size of Chicago every two-and-a-half years, filled with kids who never finished high school, no-hopers, pregnant teenagers and kids on drugs, push-outs as well as drop-outs. A city the size of Chicago. Why isn't there a sense of urgency? I mean, people are going to meetings.[12]

Haberman's last sentence seems illogical, but it really hits home to those of us who attended one endless meeting after another, participated in symposiums and seminars, served on task forces, and spent countless hours in a host of other venues. I share his frustration since rarely has anything substantive resulted from all these efforts. All the grousing and griping and hand-wringing have served no other purpose than to keep us from embarking on a new and more effective path. They have helped us maintain a bunker mentality, to keep us firmly entrenched in a safety net that protects us as individuals but abandons those in dire need of some-one—anyone—to demonstrate some leadership on their behalf.

NOTES

1. Humboldt Literacy Project, "Fast Facts on Literacy from the National Institute for Literacy," www.eurekawebs.com/humlit/fast_facts.htm.

2. Sweet, *Illiteracy: An Incurable Disease or Education Malpractice?*, www.nrrf.org/essay_Illiteracy.html.

3. Moretti, "Crime and the Costs of Criminal Justice," 146.

4. Moretti, "Crime and the Costs of Criminal Justice," 153–54.

5. Shanahan, *Children of the Code*, author's transcription from video.

6. Tedrow, "Are American Public Schools Inherently Biased?," *Teacher Magazine*, July 16, 2008, www.teachermagazine.org/tm/index.html.

7. Whitehurst, interview, *Children of the Code*, www.childrenofthecode.org/interviews/whitehurst.htm.

8. "The Library Crisis," *The Wonder of Reading*, www.wonderofreading.org/statistics.htm.

9. National Assessment of Educational Progress (NAEP), 2007 Report. According to the NAEP, "Fourth-grade students performing at the *Basic* level should demonstrate an understanding of the overall meaning of what they read. When reading text appropriate for fourth-graders, they should be able to make relatively obvious connections between the text and their own experiences and extend the ideas in the text by making simple inferences."

10. Brunner, "Reduced Recidivism and Increased Employment Opportunity through Research-Based Reading Instruction."

11. Chung, Little, Steinberg, and Altschuler, "Juvenile Justice and the Transition to Adulthood," 20.

12. Haberman, *Children of the Code*, author's transcription from video.

8

⌒♈⌒

The Unkindest Cut of All: Reading Science and the Judas Principle

"Intolerance betrays want of faith in one's cause."

—Gandhi

As we've just been reminded, early literacy is one of the most power-ful predictors of school success, gainful employment, and societal adjustment. For that reason, the sincerest expression of child advocacy that schools can offer their students is to take whatever steps are neces-sary to make proficient readers of every child. And since teachers lie at the heart of that effort, one cannot advocate for children without advo-cating for them also.

Indeed, if we are going to entrust teachers with such an awesome re-sponsibility, it would seem we would want to lend them as much support as possible. Certainly this involves favorable wages, hours, and working conditions, and the kind of respect we normally afford others who spend four or five years of postsecondary education preparing for their careers. But society doesn't seem willing to provide teachers that same kind of professional courtesy. Instead, we complain about their salaries and short work-year; we bash them for exercising their due process rights; and we assign them the lion's share of the blame when test scores decline.

READING ACHIEVEMENT: A SHARED RESPONSIBILITY

Don't get me wrong. I am not looking to sanctify teachers, nor am I seek-ing to absolve them of their responsibilities. Most teachers, in fact, would resent such an effort. My purpose, instead, is to raise awareness of the fact that, while teachers have the most direct contact with children, they cannot guarantee our children's literacy futures entirely on their own. We often read reports that reflect negatively on teacher performance, but rarely do we inquire about the practices of those who trained them or pay much attention to the job performance of those who hired them and whose role it is to support them with ongoing professional development.

This is a gross miscarriage of justice since those other constituencies do not share equally in the work nor must they deal with the level of multitasking that society seems to take for granted from its teacher ranks. Yes, of course, there are many whose jobs require attention to multiple details at the same time. But none I know of must do so while managing a classroom full of children who look to their teachers to zip their jackets, wipe their noses, referee their conflicts, assuage their hurt feelings, deal with their intransigence, and—oh yes, I almost forgot—teach them how to read and achieve at high levels.

To all this, add the fact that many perform these tasks while at the same time dealing with the ramifications of domestic abuse, neighborhood violence, an illicit drug culture, parental non-involvement, and abject poverty. For these teachers, simply getting through the day without a major incident detracting from their academic focus can be a major accomplishment in itself.

I'm sure there are some who do complain about these conditions, but rarely did I encounter any. Most assumed it all just went with the territory and, in some cases, had actively pursued careers where the challenges were most significant. But these individuals must be able to trust in those responsible for preparing them to meet those obligations and have confidence (as do those in other fields) that their training is based on the purest and most unassailable expressions of scientific inquiry. How else could we expect them to routinely develop lessons with the most explicit and unequivocal links to student achievement?

During the course of researching this book, I found that we have betrayed teachers in this regard by showing a willingness to assign them a disproportionate share of accountability—to cast them, so to speak, as the default scapegoats, not only for children's reading deficiencies, but for school failure in general.

The roots of that betrayal lie in choosing to ignore a unifying message in favor of ideological biases. That might salve some people's egos, but it is downright treachery to teachers and their pupils. As Robert Glaser, former president of the National Academy of Education, wrote back in 1985 in the foreword to *Becoming a Nation of Readers*:

> Knowledge about the intricacies of the reading process lay [sic] to rest once and for all some of the old debates about the roles of phonics and compre-

hension. We now know that learning efficient word recognition and grasping meaning are companion skills from the time a child first reads.[1]

In other words, there is no longer a need for competing pedagogies to eviscerate one another and thereby compromise their respective efforts. But there is a crying need to empower teachers by giving them training that reflects the entirety of scientific endeavors. There is that need, but it is one that continues to go unfulfilled.[2]

The data stream prior to Glaser's remarks had been vast, continuous, and methodologically pure. Succeeding generations of research compilations have proven to be even more so. But, despite these results, and the mutually beneficial relationship that has been exposed through them, conflicts over implementation have continued to rage right down to the present time. The ensuing battles have left children as collateral damage, victims of those with self-serving agendas that detract from the real goal.

But it is not just children who are victimized. Teachers are, too. While a restive public and the strictures of No Child Left Behind breathe ever more heavily down teachers' backs, those whose job it is to prepare them see neither the need nor the urgency to modify the services they offer their clients. The result is that the unifying research message has failed to gain traction in American classrooms, children continue to fail at a prodigious rate, and those who are responsible can offer nothing remotely close to the same kind of empirically derived evidence that supports practices they oppose so vehemently.

If you think all this is an overreaction or a misstatement of principles, consider the findings of a recent study by the National Council on Teacher Quality (NCTQ). (See also pp. 18 and 61.) This study found that reading research does not drive reading practice. The NCTQ looked at the syllabi of reading methods courses from a representative sampling of schools of education across the country. Among its findings:

- Only 15 percent of schools were found to teach all the components of the science of reading.
- Characteristics such as national accreditation did not increase the likelihood that an education school was more likely to teach the science of reading.
- Much of current reading instruction is incompatible with the science.
- Teacher educators portray the science of reading instruction as one approach that is no more valid than others.
- A full third made no mention of reading science whatsoever.[3]

(See figure 8.1)

MOST EDUCATION SCHOOLS ARE
NOT TEACHING THE SCIENCE OF READING

Almost all of the seventy-two institutions in our sample earned a "failing" grade, even though a passing grade was possible if a professor devoted less than 20 percent of the lectures to the science of reading. Institutions could receive a passing score if course materials merely referenced each of the five components of good reading instruction—without our knowing for certain if the science was taught correctly or adequately.

Education schools that provided exposure to all five components received a score of 100 percent, while schools that taught only one out [of] five components received a score of 20 percent. Schools that taught none of the five components received a zero. Some schools failed but their total score could not be computed because of missing or unavailable data.

Even after we set the bar for passing so low, only eleven out of seventy-two institutions (15 percent) were found to actually teach all the components of the science of reading.

Nearly a third of the institutions make no reference to reading science in any of their reading courses, even though many of these institutions require up to four reading courses.

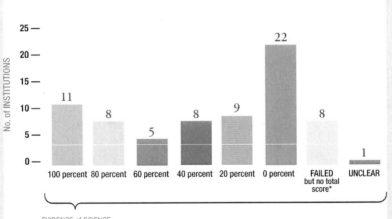

Figure 8.1

National Council on Teacher Quality. Reprinted with permission

The NCTQ report rang true in light of my experience. Obtaining my degrees and maintaining my licenses required that I take dozens of courses and attend countless staff development activities over the course of some thirty-five years. And yet until the very end of my career when I began looking into these matters on my own, I had never heard of Chall or Adams or Snow. I do remember receiving a copy of the National Reading Panel report, but I cannot recall any ongoing training sessions that ever addressed its recommendations relative to phonemic awareness and phonics despite the extensive treatment of those elements by the panel.

Reports such as *A Nation at Risk* and *Becoming a Nation of Readers* had come down to me through television news, newspapers, and magazine accounts. But I cannot recall one single instance in which I was advised to supplement holistic methods with alphabetic training. My experience was pretty much as the NCTQ report had indicated: *Schools of education did not teach reading science.*

Excerpts from an interview with Dr. G. Reid Lyon, former chief of the Child Development and Behavior Branch, National Institute of Child Health and Human Development, National Institute of Health from *Children of the Code*. Reprinted with permission.

THE DISCONNECT

But here's the disconnect and this is ironic: we obviously work with a lot of colleges and universities and we're on campuses doing a lot of studies. One of the things some of our studies do is look at the interactions that occur between moms and dads and kids. When you look at professors working with their kids from birth onward, they're reading to those kids from day one, typically. They are not only reading, but as they read even at six months of age they're pointing out the letters and the sounds. They're getting the kids to see the relationships between letters and sounds and vocabulary and concepts; they're extending language. They do it on the lap; they do it at bed-time; they do it at the dinner table. They have magnetic letters on the refrigerator. What they're doing is building not only a knowledge of language and print and how all of that goes together, but they're building brain. We can see kids who don't have these interactions and they show us brain development substantially different from kids who do have these interactions.

Now what is surprising is that a lot of these folks who interact with their kids in a very good nurturing environment and who do a lot of good systematic teaching from birth to five will then go into their undergraduate and graduate courses and teach their students never to do that. They teach their students never to do it because it's not developmentally appropriate. That's the disconnect.

The fact of the matter is, when we do our studies and we identify kids at risk for reading failure, we know that the majority of those kids who are at risk and who will hit the wall as they learn to read are kids from poverty. They are kids from disadvantaged families whose parents are working too hard to interact in the ways I just described, who may themselves not read, where there may not be books in the home. These parents may not even know they're supposed to interact with their kids that way.

We have early childhood programs where the kids go and develop good social competencies and emotional health, but the programs are bereft of any kinds of systematic interactions to do what middle and upper-middle class parents do all of the time, and the social and the emotional positives that come out of that nurturing environment go straight downhill once those kids get in school and do not learn to read.

. . . The bottom line is for a country like America to be leaving behind about thirty-eight to 40 percent of its youngsters in terms of not learning to read is unconscionable.

* * *

PROPAGANDIZED

My toughest challenge is not so much the science anymore. The toughest challenge we have is in moving the science to the development of teachers and their preparation, such that what they learn is actually objective and is based upon converging evidence rather than philosophies, belief systems, or appeals to authority. We need to get the information to teachers who have been, in a sense, propagandized into these very broad and general and non-evidentiary kinds of approaches that they use in teaching reading—absolute failures in terms of our scientific tests vis-à-vis their effectiveness.

When I was a teacher I wanted to get up every morning and make a difference in kids' lives, and when I saw I wasn't making a difference in kids' lives that hurt the kids. But it also made me feel dumb, foolish, embarrassed. Our teachers sometimes feel the same way, but they can only teach what they've been taught, typically.

Teachers come to these very complex interactions, to teach reading for example, with a very limited set of knowledge modules, if you will, a very limited set of concepts in terms of how kids learn to read.

* * *

The resistance in the educational community, particularly at the higher education level where teachers are trained, is enormous, almost unbelievable.

LEAVE NO TEACHER BEHIND

As I stated earlier, most teachers do not spend their time wringing their hands and bemoaning their fate. They press forward with remarkable resolve, reaching to find their own answers when all else has failed. But that is a formidable task when the conventional wisdom related to reading instruction has left them out in the cold. In medicine, research guides practice. But the same cannot be said for reading instruction. Withholding the product of legitimate science—and then blaming teachers when children fail—is, as Julius Caesar (or, at least, the Bard himself) would have put it, *the unkindest cut of all*.

Meeting society's expectations for children is a challenge teachers gladly accept. However, it is a shared responsibility, one requiring that other elements of the reading community fulfill their respective roles as well. In that regard, schools of education and district personnel must be as accountable to teachers as teachers are to their students. If there is to be legislation that purports to leave no child behind, then we must do the same for teachers; we must not leave even one of them behind by failing to arm them with the full range of the scientific enterprise.

But that is exactly what we do when we continue to pursue unverified and thereby ill-fated tangents, then leave them hanging in the wind when such methods prove worthless. Proceeding on such questionable grounds sets education back to the days when leeches and garlic cloves were deemed appropriate strategies to ward off infection. If we are going to demand accountability from teachers, we owe them the tools that give them the best chance for success. Failing to do so represents the ultimate betrayal.

NOTES

1. Glaser, "Foreword," *Becoming a Nation of Readers*, vi.
2. Reschly, Holdheide, Smartt, and Oliver, *Evaluation of LBS-I Teacher Preparation in Inclusive Practices, Reading and Classroom Organization-Behavior Management*.
3. Walsh, Glaser, and Wilcox, Executive Summary, *What Education Schools Aren't Teaching about Reading and What Elementary Teachers Aren't Learning*, 4, 7–8.

9

⋰⋱

The 3 Rs:
Reform, Reform, Reform

"Every reform, however necessary, will by weak minds be carried to an excess, that itself will need reforming."

—Samuel Taylor Coleridge

Educators may not have been inclined to pursue research-based practices to any measurable degree, but they have proved remarkably persistent in other ways. Indeed, if there is anything that has defined their efforts over the past several decades, it is the endless drive to develop and engage in innovative practices.

During that time, we have seen one reform measure after another cross the stage, bow to an adoring audience, then exit stage left as the newest messianic measure takes its turn in the limelight. The following are but a few examples: authentic pedagogy and assessment, brain-based teaching and learning, core knowledge, cultural literacy, didactic teaching, emotional intelligence, global education, inquiry-based teaching, learning styles, multiple intelligences, outcome-based education, alternative assessment, school-based management, school-to-work movement, self-esteem movement, Socratic questioning, thematic curriculum, and countless others that publishers and curriculum designers churn out day after day.

That is not to demean any particular one. Many of these reforms—many, but not all—are laudable in intent, were developed by dedicated and highly trained individuals, and reflect sound educational practice. But they come and go with such rapidity, and reflect such a wide swath of philosophical underpinnings, it is often difficult to know whether their use represents cutting-edge practice or practice that undercuts the development of skills necessary to benefit from them. One author who has made a career of studying school reform stated in an interview:

> The reforms tend not to get discarded but, rather, to layer atop one another, or at least to leave a residue. Of course that can also lead to highly confusing multilayered endeavors with no real clear focus and a surfeit of checks-and-balances, categorical funding constraints, over-specialized people, and more.[1]

And, despite the fact that we have been innovating for decades, publishers and curriculum designers continue to feed the insatiable desire of schools and districts to be perceived as leaders in school reform. The need to be seen in this light is so important that innovation appears to have supplanted achievement as the cause célèbre. When reading performance, for example, continues to drop, the response is often to appease the public with a new blueprint, new accountability measures, new standards, new improvement plans, new ways to elicit involvement, new everything—all of which promise to stop the bleeding and turn things around.

In the introduction to their book, *A Critical Thinker's Guide to Educational Fads: How to Get Beyond Educational Glitz and Glitter*, Dr. Richard Paul and Dr. Linda Elder write:

> The history of education is also the history of educational panaceas, the comings and goings of quick fixes for deep-seated educational problems. This old problem is dramatically on the increase. The result is intensifying fragmentation of energy and effort in the schools, together with a significant waste of time and money. Many teachers become increasingly cynical and jaded.[2]

It is like a fading movie star who constantly seeks to reinvent himself in a way that will make him more marketable to a wider audience. The difference is that, eventually, he must settle on something and remain with it long enough to determine whether it has indeed worked. That last point is apparently lost on many in education. Teachers are bombarded so frequently with new ways to address their students' learning needs that they are often hard-pressed to know at any given point what exactly has been added and what they should maintain or reject from the past.

The focus on standards-based practices was supposed to help with that effort by lending some specificity not only to what was to be taught, but also how teachers might go about teaching it. But there has been little uniformity in that regard. A study by the Rand Corporation found that there was little cohesiveness among staffs regarding how they chose to address the achievement goals necessary to meet accountability standards. The researchers found that, when the data were analyzed for consistency, educators' responses varied more within individual schools than they did between schools or districts.[3]

Some analysts say the findings suggest that the efforts of many district and school leaders to align educator professional development with content standards have not consistently translated into the kind of instructional changes that standards-based reforms are intended to inspire. Those include the increased use of test data to shape what happens in the classroom.

"I think a lot of districts are really very concerned about NCLB," said Kerstin Le Floch, a principal research analyst at the Washington-based American Institutes of Research, who has studied the implementation of the 2002 law. "But somehow there's some disconnect in the linkages between central district offices and schools."[4]

D'ya think?

Consider the matter of "balanced literacy," a program that supposedly was created to assuage those who objected to a lack of phonological treatment in early reading programs. In 2003, a year after New York fourth-graders had shown significant progress in reading, the superintendent awarded multimillion-dollar contracts to provide balanced literacy training to teachers in the city's eight hundred elementary schools. The following is a description of the results after five years:

> Last fall, the federal government released the latest test results from the National Assessment of Educational Progress—and they showed that New York City students made no progress in reading in fourth grade or eighth grade from 2003 to 2007.
>
> On the federal test, there were no significant gains in reading for black students, white students, Hispanic students, Asian students, or lower-income students. Forty-three percent of fourth-graders in New York City were "below basic"—the lowest possible rating.[5]

Even though balanced literacy remains in place in New York today, the superintendent has since suggested it might be wise to try something else. He has recommended for primary-age children adoption of a program called "core knowledge," which integrates content knowledge, phonics, and vocabulary.[6]

What? Is this to suggest that balanced literacy didn't cover those things in the first place? Evidently not, as the results have shown. How then could it be described as "balanced?"

MORE TIME FOR DOUGHNUTS

As a teacher, I recall a day in the school calendar set aside for staff development. After we all had our doughnuts, a district curriculum specialist began his presentation. Barely a minute had passed when another district official interrupted the proceedings to have a private conversation with the presenter. After a few minutes had elapsed, we were told that the event was canceled and we were free to work in our classrooms for the remainder of the day. My understanding was that this scenario had played itself out at several other sites.

It was like a squadron of paratroopers whose mission was canceled at the eleventh hour because someone discovered a design flaw in everyone's ripcord. All of us wondered exactly what had happened, but a specific explanation was not forthcoming. My interpretation, therefore, is personal and speculative. Evidently, someone discovered that the program about to be presented to staffs had fallen into disfavor in some circles. Implementing it would have put us at odds with the latest theoretical advances and tarnished our reputation as a district. Whether the decision to pull it was made by an individual or by committee is anyone's guess, but the result was that days, perhaps months, of preparation by staff development professionals were rendered utterly useless.

AN EDUCATOR'S GUIDE TO REFORM

All this might be excused if we could show that most of these novel approaches actually worked. But that has hardly been the case. The American Institute for Research once conducted a study entitled *An Educator's Guide to Schoolwide Reform*. The study examined twenty-four reform models that had been initiated over the previous ten years. It found that a third of them offered no evidence whatsoever of any relationship between their respective dynamic and actual achievement. The investigators also had a difficult time identifying research among the others that was rigorous enough to make any legitimate statistical comparisons.

Seven did include appropriate experiments, but they were few in number (two or three) and their correlations to improvement were anemic. Using "weak," "marginal," "promising," and "strong" as descriptors of a relationship to achievement, six of the aforementioned seven were deemed as marginal and the remaining one as weak. Only two among the entire group had more than five studies stringent enough to satisfy the investigators' criteria. One was Direct Instruction (fourteen studies), the other Success for All (fifteen). The relationships between those two programs and actual achievement were described as strong.[7] See complete results and explanatory information beginning on page 101. This is not something we need to fear in other fields where clinical studies and codified results must be present before a product or a procedure is placed on the market. The weak links to achievement of the vast majority of these programs notwithstanding, they somehow still managed to make their ways into thousands of schools across the country at an aggregate cost that must lie somewhere in the nine-figure range.

Medical practitioners refuse to even consider treatments that don't have clinical evidence to vouch for their safety. Why should education be any different, given that a lifetime of illiteracy or low literacy is as damaging to an individual as any other threat, medical or otherwise?

Following are graphic representations of the results of *An Educator's Guide to Schoolwide Reform*.

Twenty-Four School Reform Approaches at a Glance
The table on pages 104 and 105 summarizes the reviews of all twenty-four schoolwide approaches.

The information it provides is limited. To fully understand the ratings, readers are encouraged to review the profiles. The table provides a snapshot of the information that was available at the time this guide was prepared. Developers continue to modify and strengthen the approaches and to gather and report information on their effectiveness.

(The table is reprinted with permission. Herman, Rebecca. 1999. *An Educators' Guide to Schoolwide Reform.* Prepared by American Institute for Research, Rebecca Herman, Project Director. Arlington, VA: Educational Research Services.)

Reading the Table
The table presents information in five areas: evidence of positive effects on student achievement; year each approach was introduced in schools; number of schools using the approaches; support developers provide schools; and first-year adoption costs (high and low estimates).

Approaches are rated in two of these areas: evidence of positive effects on student achievement, and support developers provide schools. A full circle (●) indicates a strength. An empty circle (○) indicates a weakness. The half-filled circle (◑) suggests promise, and the quarter circle (◔) indicates a marginal rating. The question mark (?) indicates that the research evidence is so limited that there really is no evidence on which to assess effects on student achievement or the support the developer provides schools.

The table can be read by rows and by columns. For example, the row on *Support Developer Provides Schools* indicates that the developers of twelve approaches provide schools with "strong" implementation support. Ten developers provide "promising" support for implementation, and two provide "marginal" support.

The columns in the table provide an at-a-glance summary of each approach. For example, the column on Core Knowledge indicates that schools have used this approach since 1990. There are currently seven hundred and fifty Core Knowledge schools. A review of the studies that have examined Core Knowledge schools indicates it has "promising" evidence of effects on student achievement, provides schools with "promising" support for implementation, and is moderately expensive to put in place.

To the right side of the table, the column on Talent Development High School indicates that ten schools are using this approach, which was first introduced to schools in 1994. Studies of Talent Development High School show "marginal" evidence of effects on students and "strong" support provided by the developer for implementation. Costs to adopt this approach are moderate.

Understanding the Ratings

Evidence of Positive Effects on Student Achievement. The first row of the table presents ratings for *Evidence of Positive Effects on Student Achievement*. Each approach is rated on a five-point scale ranging from "strong" evidence of positive effects to a "no research" rating, which indicates there are no rigorous studies on which to judge the approach's effects on student achievement. Each rating is explained in the key below.

The ratings were compiled from individual reviews of available studies, each of which was ranked according to methodological criteria such as sample size, duration of the study, appropriateness of comparison groups, and relevance of measurement instruments.

In general, evidence of positive effects on student achievement—arguably the most important feature of any reform approach—is extremely limited. Even though many of the approaches have been in schools for years, only three provide strong evidence of positive effects on student achievement. As a result, educators often are considering schoolwide reform without vital information on which to make decisions. More rigorous evaluations are needed, with broad dissemination of findings.

Support Developer Provides Schools. The fourth row of the table presents ratings for the *Support Developer Provides Schools*. This four-point rating ranges from strong implementation support, in which developers provide a range of services, to weak support, in which developers only provide initial training for school staffs. Higher ratings indicate that the developers provide access to appropriate types of support, frequent support over an extended time, and tools to help schools evaluate implementation.

Each rating is explained in the key below.

It is important to note, however, that some developers may not provide extensive support because schools do not need it to implement a particular approach successfully. To get a full picture of what kinds of changes are required of schools and what kinds of support are offered, readers should compare profiles.

Ratings of Evidence of Positive Effects
on Student Achievement
● = **Strong evidence of positive effects on student achievement**
A *strong* rating indicates that four or more studies, using rigorous methodologies, show some positive effects on student achievement, with

at least three of such studies showing effects that are educationally (or statistically) significant. Further, only 20 percent of studies show negative or no effects on students. To ensure enough information for future replications, at least one study provides information on implementation as well as on effects.

◑ = Promising evidence of positive effects on student achievement
A *promising* rating indicates that three or more studies, using rigorous methodologies, show positive effects of the approach on student achievement, with at least one such study showing effects at statistically or educationally significant levels. No more than 30 percent of studies show negative or no effects on students, and at least one study provides information on implementation. Evidence that is rated as *promising*, rather than *strong*, may include fewer studies using rigorous methodologies, fewer studies showing significant effects, or a higher proportion of studies showing negative or no effects.

◕ = Marginal evidence of positive effects on student achievement
A *marginal* rating indicates that at least one study, using rigorous methodology, shows positive effects of the approach on student achievement. At least 50 percent of studies show positive effects on student achievement. Evidence that is rated marginal rather than promising may include fewer studies using rigorous methodologies, fewer studies showing significant effects, or a higher proportion of studies showing negative or no effects.

○ = Evidence of mixed, weak, or no effects on student achievement
A *mixed, weak, or no effects* rating indicates that at least one study, using rigorous methodology, shows negative or no effects of the approach on student achievement. Evidence that is rated *mixed, weak, or no effects* rather than *marginal* may include the same number and quality of studies, but the findings are negative or ambiguous rather than positive.

? = No research on effects on student achievement
A *no research* rating indicates there are no methodologically rigorous studies by which to assess effects of the approach on student achievement.

REFORMATION REVISITED

I have a teacher friend who was leader of a group that responded to a call for innovative school proposals by submitting a plan for the district's high schools. The proposal called for the establishment of schools with the authority to enforce but two requirements: students would need to attend at a minimum rate of eighty percent and commit no violent acts on school premises. The proposal was summarily rejected.

The point of mentioning this is to show that true reform lies somewhere other than where we have looked. As we have seen in the case of

Summary Table of All 24 Approaches

	Evidence of positive effects on student achievement[2]	Year introduced in schools	Number of schools	Support developer provides schools	First year costs[3]	First-year costs with current staff reassigned
Accelerated Schools (K–8)	◕	'86	1000	◐	$27	$14
America's Choice (K–12)	?	'98	300	●	$190	$90
ATLAS Communities (PreK–12)	?	'92	63	◐	$98	$90
Audrey Cohen College (K–12)	?	'70	16	◐	$161	$86
Basic Schools Network (K–12)	?	'92	150	◐	$12	NC
Coalition of Essential Schools (K–12)	○	'84	1000	◕	NA	NA
Community for Learning (K–12)	◐	'90	92	●	$157	$82
Co-NECT (K–12)	?	'92	75	●	$588	NC
Core Knowledge (K–8)	◐	'90	750	◐	$56	NC
Different Ways of Knowing (K–7)	◐	'89	412	●	$84	NC
Direct Instruction (K–6)	●	Late 60's	150	◐	$244	$194
Expeditionary Learning Outward Bound (K–12)	◐	'92	65	●	$81	NC
The Foxfire Fund (K–12)	?	'66	NA	◕	$65	NC
High Schools That Work (9–12)	●	'87	860	●	$48	NC

Program	Evidence[2]	Year	Schools		Cost[3]	NC
High/Scope (K–3)	◑ (Marginal)	'67	27	●	$130[4]	NC
League of Professional Schools (K–12)	◑ (Marginal)	'89	158	◐	$13	NC
Modern Red Schoolhouse (K–12)	?	'93	50	●	$215	NC
Onward to Excellence (K–12)	◑ (Marginal)	'81	1000	●	$72	$60
Paideia (K–12)		'82	80	◐	$146	$96
Roots and Wings (PreK–6)	◑ (Marginal)	'93	200	●	$270	$70
School Development Program (K–12)	◐ (Promising)	'68	700	◐	$45	$32
Success for All (PreK–6)	● (Strong)	'87	1130	●	$270	$70
Talent Development High School (9–12)	◑ (Marginal)	'94	10	●	$57	$27
Urban Learning Centers (PreK–12)	?	'93	13	◐	$169	$159

● = Strong ◐ = Promising ◑ = Marginal ○ = Mixed, Weak

[1] This table summarizes information from *An Educator's Guide to Schoolwide Reform*.
[2] Although many types of student outcomes are important, evidence of positive effects on student achievement is a key consideration in selecting schoolwide reforms.
However, some schools may wish to consider a new approach that has not yet developed strong evidence of effectiveness, but provides the strongest match with school goals.
[3] Costs are in thousand of dollars (e.g., $62=$62,000).
[4] The estimate for High/Scope assumes a school of 25 K–3 teachers.

reading instruction, we can do a million different things in an effort to bolster performance. But their potential is limited at best unless we establish requisite skills to carry them out. And, therefore, reform measures must address those issues first. Johnny can't succeed unless we can guarantee that he masters the ability to decode words and interpret text, just as high schools will have a hard time showing results if students don't attend or if we cannot guarantee a safe environment for all.

It's like suggesting that, if we would like a young piano student to someday show creative interpretation of a magnificent concerto, it might be a good idea if he or she first knew what all those notes meant. Would it not be reasonable to conclude that those who had mastered the relationship between the notes on the page and the sounds they represented would be more likely than not to go on to become better piano players than those who hadn't?

It is hard to imagine that, in our infinite quest to serve children better, we have somehow lost sight of that rudimentary precept. It is hard to imagine, given that we were once at a point where the rate of illiteracy was so low it was assumed that it was just a matter of time before it would be wiped out entirely. And it is hard to imagine, given that pure and applied science has been pointing this out to us for over five decades. Before we try to reform anything, why don't we first reform ourselves by overcoming those forces that want to keep us from discovering answers that lie right under our collective noses.

NOTES

1. Finn, Princeton University Press, transcript of interview, March 5, 2008.

2. Paul and Elder, *A Critical Thinker's Guide to Educational Fads*, 4.

3. Fuller and Hannum, *Strong States, Weak Schools: The Benefits and Dilemmas of Centralized Accountability*.

4. Sawchuk, "Leadership Gap Seen in Post-NCLB Changes in U.S. Teachers," www.edweek.org/ew/index.html.

5. Klein, "Right on Reading: NYC Schools Finally Get Smart," September 1, 2008.

6. The Core Knowledge Foundation, coreknowledge.org/.

7. Herman, *An Educators' Guide to Schoolwide Reform*, www.aasa.org/issues_ insights/district_organization/Reform/overview.htm.

10

꒰ఎ꒱

Teaching to Mastery

"We are what we repeatedly do. Excellence, therefore, is not an act but a habit."

—Aristotle

Why has the research message failed to catch on? Why is there such a disconnect between quantified theory building and educational practice? Perhaps a good way to answer those questions is to look at a program that applies the scientific findings with rigor and precision and to then use that information to explain why it is something we don't normally see happening in classrooms.

To accomplish this, I will expound upon how a particular program known as *Reading Mastery* (RM), one of several core programs known as direct instruction (DI), incorporates the spirit of the empirical evidence. I choose RM for this purpose because it is the one with which I am most familiar, having researched it at length, implemented it in my own school, and seen its use in multiple venues. This association allows me to describe it in my own words rather than using any of the publisher's promotional materials.[1]

I will begin by depicting a typical lesson and follow that up with descriptions of four key elements: time on task, scripted lessons, behavior management, and program monitoring. I wish to make it clear, however, that these elements are just part of what goes into an effective implementation.

Chapter 10

TYPICAL LESSON

In a typical first-grade lesson, the teacher holds up a book containing letters and/or phonemes. She points to one of them and models the correct pronunciation. The class must demonstrate the three elements of a correct answer: (1) *all* must respond, (2) *all* must respond in unison, and (3) *all* must respond correctly. To facilitate this and to keep the lesson moving along at an acceptable rate, the teacher can use various signaling devices such as hand clapping, finger snapping, or tapping the book. If the group does not meet all three conditions for a correct answer, the teacher must repeat the prompt until it does. Normally, a correct answer can be elicited on the first try but in many instances two or more may be required. This same procedure used to build phonics mastery is also used to reinforce correct recitation of sentences, paragraphs, and stories when students advance to those levels.

Regardless of the stage at which a group is functioning, maintaining focus by everyone is essential. Normally, a more distractible child is positioned directly in front of the teacher. This makes it virtually impossible for that student to lose concentration without being immediately detected. In most cases, simple eye contact or a furrowed brow is enough to refocus an individual without ever losing a second's worth of learning time. But even that is considered negative reinforcement, something to be avoided as much as possible. That same furrowed brow can be changed to a smile and a nod when a child is performing admirably. In addition, teachers are expected to sprinkle behavior-specific positive comments throughout: "Way to answer all together," or "We could put this to music," or "That's five correct responses in a row; I'll bet you can do ten."

To assure that no one is slipping under the radar, the teacher will at times elicit a response from an individual child. This keeps them all vigilant since they realize that they may be called upon at any given moment. It also informs the teacher about individual mastery. When a child fails to answer correctly, the teacher doesn't wait endlessly for a correct response. She can return to that same child a few seconds later after having the group or other individuals model the correct answer a few more times. A skillful teacher directs this procedure like a maestro, artfully, productively, and respectfully, while the children advance with unrelenting resolve.

Mastery of all concepts is essential—minute-to-minute, day-to-day, and week-to-week. The teacher must not only know at once that a particular child is not performing satisfactorily, but also she must be prepared to deal with it immediately. Allowing a child to languish without improvement until the next quarter or marking period translates to a loss of days, even months. Strategies for these cases can include repeating or "firming up" a lesson so, the next day, the child can pick up commensurate with his classmates. Educational assistants and other qualified professionals can fill this role in accordance with proper licensing and union contracts.

In some instances, when a child is improperly placed, it may be necessary to move him or her back a series of lessons by reassigning him to a group that has not yet advanced to that level. It doesn't mean the child is dull or challenged or incapable. It merely indicates he was improperly placed to begin with and must proceed from his appropriate level of functioning. By the same token, those who are having too easy a time can, and should, be advanced to higher levels.

TIME ON TASK

With RM, the reading period is sacrosanct. I know everybody will claim that theirs is too, but never have I found a program that manifests that characteristic to such an extensive degree. Reading must occur on each and every one of the allotted days in the school calendar. While things like field trips, holiday celebrations, and school programs certainly play an essential role in a child's overall school experience, such activities must never occur at the expense of the day's reading lesson. *Never.*

Within the context of the lesson itself, teachers must take draconian measures so as not to squander any of the allocated learning time. If the reading period is scheduled to start at 8:30 a.m., then it must commence at exactly that moment, earlier if possible. This doesn't mean that children are to begin moving to their assigned locations at that time, while they have conversations with friends, search for materials, or take the attendance folder to the office. It means that they are seated in front of their teacher and ready to respond to his or her prompts. Once begun, directed teaching must not end until the requisite amount of time has elapsed. Successfully completing a lesson is not cause for a break but rather an opportunity to move forward to the next one.

Those who work in classrooms know this doesn't happen magically. Students as well as adults are often slow to transition from one location or activity to another. Therefore, the expectation that one will be ready to learn at a specified moment must be established through discipline and practice. Teachers who experience the most success with the program rehearse transitioning procedures on day one and maintain rigorous standards throughout the year.

I would invite those who believe it is unnecessary to use such measures to track the numbers. Use a stopwatch to record when teaching begins and stop it each time something interrupts its progression. Ed Schaefer of Educational Associates looked at these numbers for a typical school during a typical school year of 180 six-and-a-half-hour days, or a total of 1,170 hours. He found that student absence and non-instructional periods such as lunch and recess reduce the number of hours designated for teaching and learning to about 835. Administrative tasks, transitions, discipline, etc., eat up another 209 hours, leaving just 626 hours for actual instruction.

But experience tells us that it doesn't end there, since children are not always on task. A typical school's students will show an engagement rate of seventy-five percent, which cuts learning time another 157 hours, leaving just 469 in which to cover all the content areas. But even if students are engaged, that doesn't mean they are engaged successfully. They may not understand what is being taught or they may be involved in the inaccurate completion of assigned tasks. Schaefer finds that students in a typical school lose about twenty-five percent of their learning time due to inaccurate participation. When you do the math, a picture emerges revealing that active, gainful learning occurs for just over two hours per day, or less than a third of the time students spend in school.[2]

I realize it is not realistic to think that we can accurately engage students during designed instructional periods 100 percent of the time. But some do a better job than others. This is borne out by Schaefer's comparisons of a *typical* school to an *effective* school. An effective school, he found, keeps non-instructional time to a minimum. And, perhaps of even greater importance, effective schools increase the engagement rate of pupils during actual teaching from seventy-five percent to ninety percent and, at the same time, increase the success rate while engaged from eighty percent to ninety percent. This is certainly not perfect, but schools that can manage to do it can squeeze an additional two hundred hours of academic learning time out of the school year, which translates to over an hour more per day of accurately engaged activity.

Remember, proficiency by the end of the primary grades is a critical plateau. That additional hour means an extra 720 hours of accurately engaged learning time between kindergarten and the end of third grade. To contend that it is critical is in no way to overstate the case.

It is small wonder, then, that RM focuses so heavily on maintaining the integrity of the directed reading lesson. Engaging children successfully at a ninety percent level during the specified reading lesson, and using clinically tested measures while doing so, can and will yield the desired goal—on-level readers. These results can be achieved under even the most challenging circumstances if teachers have the requisite training and are vigilant in carrying it out every day. Remember, I am referring specifically in this context to the reading lesson. I am not suggesting that we subject students to such intense participation and oversight throughout the entire day. But, when it comes to achieving that most essential of all skills—reading level mastery—nothing can be left to chance. Failure in that regard cannot be an option.

But time on task is only part of what it means to be direct and systematic or, as the data would suggest, research-based.

THE SCRIPT

Teachers using RM follow a script and are expected to rehearse it before meeting with the group so they can apply it as directed. Fidelity to the script, its structure, the pacing, the sequencing, the prompting, etc., have all been tested in actual classrooms and found to be most effective, so it is essential that teachers follow it to the letter. They may, at times, add to it, but only if the addition is relevant to the skill at hand.

A good share of the reading community has a difficult time abiding the use of a script, scientific or otherwise. Most basals, in their teacher editions, offer a suggested sequence for addressing skills, but they are merely meant as guidelines. Teachers are expected to supplement and enrich lessons using their own creative instincts. Constructivists contend that this is what makes a reading lesson effective. Research-based practitioners would respond by saying, "Yeah? Prove it." That is not to be smug. It is just meant to convey the idea that we cannot expect teachers to pull verifiably cogent activities off the top of their heads day in and day out, regardless of how skillful any one of them might be.

THE CHASM

This is just one expression of the philosophical chasm that exists between the two constructs and perhaps one of the main reasons research-based practices have not been implemented in the recommended fashion. It's like the two are separated by a time warp. The constructivist response to research that suggests that teachers reading from a script and eliciting repetitive responses from children is in their best interest is not merely to imply, but to state without equivocation, that there is something intrinsically wrong with the research. To them, this can't possibly be what reading is about, at least not on this planet.

What they fail to realize or consider is that the script is but a means to an end. Creative lessons designed and presented to students have far more significance for students who own the ability to decode and interpret text. Absent that skill, their participation in such activities is mainly vicarious in nature. In order to personalize the experience and derive the kind of deep knowledge that leads to the critical thinking ability we all know is so important, students must be capable of independently interpreting text, fluently and effortlessly.

I recall assigning my fifth-graders to read versions of the *Iliad* and the *Odyssey* adapted for young readers. They enjoyed the stories immensely and had a delightful time completing the integrated projects contained in the unit. What is more, they gained a jump-start in understanding ancient history and Greek mythology. But these kids were high-performing fifth-graders who long ago had managed to crack the code and meaningful interpretation of the text was never at issue.

The challenge for me, the teacher, was to get them to digest the material, relate it to their prior knowledge and experience, and use it as a springboard for creative and expository writing—in other words, foster their ability to gain exponentially from their ability to interpret the printed word. Unfortunately, there were other groups of fifth-graders who lacked the ability to gain such deep knowledge because they lacked independent word recognition strategies. Most of their effort would have to be expended merely trying to decipher those clusters of letters, leaving precious little time to make meaningful associations with the knowledge thus gained.

DISCRIMINATION?

I have heard some offer the opinion that it is discriminatory to expose poor and minority children to harsh practices such as drills and teacher scripts when we are far less likely to ask their more affluent peers to do the same. Maybe there is a disparity there, as the science does suggest that less advantaged children stand to benefit more from such practices. But what I find truly discriminatory is a condition in which some children reach their intermediate years struggling to master concepts they should have learned years earlier. That is where the discrimination lies, not in the method, but in the end result. As unsavory as scripted lessons appear to many, they seem like a small price to pay to gain the kind of high-level text interpretation that can spell the difference between school success and school failure.

BEHAVIOR MANAGEMENT

Reading Mastery requires active participation throughout the lesson, which lasts between twenty and thirty minutes. The need for disciplining squanders precious learning time, time that can never be retrieved. Therefore, teachers must position their group so that all children are within their field of vision at all times. In addition to providing positive comments for academic performance, the teacher must also reward compliant behavior: "Marcus showed Sarah where we left off. Thanks, Marcus," or "I have not had to stop once to remind someone to behave. Great job, all of you."

Negative reinforcement must be kept to a bare minimum. There may be times when this is unavoidable, but waiting until the negative behavior turns to something positive, or at least neutral, and then reinforcing that behavior forges a better relationship between student and teacher and dramatically reduces the likelihood that resentment or alienation will ensue. Another strategy is to reinforce those surrounding the nonparticipator. The message usually gets through, and attention is reestablished without losing even a second's worth of time. Pupil deportment is rarely a problem during RM lessons when teachers are skilled at using these kinds of reinforcement techniques.

I realize that some will say that these measures apply in all kinds of classroom settings and not just to a program like RM. Here again, I would not argue. However, I have yet to see a reading program that treats behavior management as a specified part of program implementation. Delivering a lesson properly means distinguishing between behavioral and academic reinforcements and taking the steps to ensure that the ratio between positive and negative comments remains high. Thus behavior management and instructional strategies are intertwined. Schools with effective implementations experience a significant drop in office referrals during the directed reading lesson.

MONITORING

Maintaining rigorous adherence to all the program's requirements is difficult work and requires frequent monitoring by school administration. Principals have a responsibility to know what an effective lesson looks like and to make daily visits to assure that that is what they are seeing. During a routine observation, she is looking for all children in the group to be on task, checking to see if the teacher is eliciting enough responses per minute, verifying that prompts are repeated until all three elements of a correct answer are present, and assuring that individual turns can confirm individual mastery. To monitor all this, the principal can use a form to tally things such as:

- Number of responses per minute
- Number of correct responses per minute
- Ratio of correct to incorrect responses
- Number of social reinforcements
- Ratio of negative to positive reinforcements

(See sample monitoring forms 10.1 and 10.2, for use by principals, literary coaches, peer coaches, etc.)

Teachers can learn to do these things relatively quickly, but refining their skills to maximum effect can take awhile and requires support at all levels. It is, therefore, the principal's responsibility to provide assistance for teachers whose program delivery is marginal or who may have inadvertently slipped into habits that compromise effectiveness. Most schools with RM or other DI programs use a literacy coach as well as a consultant. Their main role is to monitor lesson progress, model proper implementation, and keep accurate records for the principal. Even skilled practitioners benefit, since there is always room for improvement and the constant refinement of skills helps bring to children the program's full potential.

As students progress, the nature of the lessons begins to change. The emphasis on phonics diminishes as students master each concept. Ultimately, the need for phonics training no longer exists and all subsequent lessons focus entirely on text interpretation, which is, as all the major reports maintain, the ultimate purpose of learning to read. (See chapter 4.)

At this point, the constructivist recommendation of a print-rich environment now takes on so much more significance. Children can now independently read and understand so many more of the books in which they have been immersed. As they do so, they have increased their ability to build background knowledge and are much better prepared to engage in writing activities and activities that require critical thinking ability—matters so important to holistic theory. In short, they have gone from *learning to read* to being capable of *reading to learn*.

Sample Monitoring Form 10.1w.

Reading Mastery
Quick Monitoring Checklist

Teacher_____ Lesson_____ Date_____

I. Planning
☐ Clear expectations were set by teacher and followed by students.
☐ Record keeping was up-to-date and in accordance with specified procedures.
☐ Materials were organized and transitions are efficient.
☐ Seating arrangement was appropriate.
☐ Program testing was completed and recorded.
☐ Gains Charts were up-to-date and accessible to administrator.

II. Instruction
☐ Instruction started on time and continued to end of period.
☐ Formats were presented faithfully and effectively in a consistent manner.
☐ Students were monitored for accuracy, both individually and as a group.
☐ At least 90% of errors were corrected immediately.
☐ Appropriate signals were used.
☐ Pacing was appropriate to group and engaging to students.
☐ Response rate per minute was adequate.

III. Classroom Management
☐ Clear expectations were set by teacher and followed by students.
☐ Transitions were fast and efficient.
☐ Seating arrangement facilitated entire group monitoring.
☐ Low performers were seated for maximum supervision.
☐ Ratio of positive reinforcement to negative comments was 3:1 or higher.
☐ Behavior was monitored appropriately.

IV. Assessment
☐ All assessments were delivered as specified.
☐ All written records were accurate and up-to-date.
☐ Gains Charts were posted and reflected adequate progress.
☐ Remediation and retesting were administered to document mastery.
☐ Reteaching and retesting were administered when needed.
☐ Regrouping decisions were made based on student performance.

Sample Monitoring Form 10.2.

Mar/25/99	**Instruction Observation Form**	A data form of The Institute for Effective Education

Instructor: *Julianne*	Observer: *Louise*	Date: *6/15/99*
Subject/Lesson: *CNC-C, L.58*	Schedule Time Begin: *9:40* Schedule Time End: *10:30*	Scheduled Time Total: *50 min.*
Counting Period: *15 min. → beginning* Actual Time Begin: *9:50*	Actual Time End: *10:22*	Actual Time Total: *32 min.*

Student Academic Responses		Positive Consequences		Negative Consequences	
Group	**Individual**	**Praise**	**Other**	**Rules**	**Penalties**

Student Academic Responses

Group	Individual
⊕ ⊕ / / ⊕ / + ⊕	## ##
### ⊕ / ⊕ ⊕ ⊕	##
/ / + ⊕ / / ⊕ ###	//
### ###	

/ = response; + = error; ⊕ = error corrected

Positive Consequences / Negative Consequences

	Praise	Other	Rules	Penalties
Academic Performance				
	###			/
	###			
Social Performance				
	###		###	
	///		/	

Examples:

Positive	Negative
• You got it	• Wrong
• Great job	• Stay in your seat
• Excellent	• Now is not the time to sharpen your pencil

Comments

Student responses per minute:
Academic responses / minutes
57 / 15 = | **4 RPM** | OK for CMC

Percent Correct Responses:
100 x Corrects / Academic responses
100 × 45 / 57 = | **79%** | w/in instructional level

Percent Positive Consequences:
100 x Positives / (Pos. + Neg.)
100 × 18 / 25 = | **72%** **3:1** | Much improved

Percent Group responses:
Percent individual responses:
17 / 57 = | **70%** **30%** | Nice ratio

	Hi	M	Lo	
Are materials organized?	(Hi)	M	Lo	
Is Transition time quick and smooth?	Hi	(M)	Lo	Some delay between rate drill & lesson
Are students ready for lesson?	(Hi)	M	Lo	Students were ready when you arrived!
Is lesson delivered fluently?	(Hi)	M	Lo	Followed script. Enthusiastic voice.
Are errors corrected immediately?	Hi	(M)	Lo	Missed a couple of corrections
Is independent work appropriate? (class & level)	(Hi)	M	Lo	Yes
Are other students monitored?	Hi	M	Lo	N/A

- Your students knew what to do before you got there — great procedures training.
- Your % positive has increased nicely.
- Be careful — a couple of errors got by you.
- I recommend that you do more signal training w/your group — some errors could have been avoided.
- RPM were "OK" considering there were written responses too.
- Work on maximizing your instructional time by teaching transition procedures. This will also help with your transitions with the class. → out of 50 min. period → instructional time = 34 min. Transitions = 18 min.
- Your lesson was enthusiastically delivered. Looked like fun!

Reprinted with permission from the Institute for Effective Education.

DIRECT AND SYSTEMATIC: CAN IT GAIN FULL ACCEPTANCE?

Many today claim that their programs are balanced and reflect the research dynamic. However, I would maintain that few do so with the intensity and the precision and the attention to detail as that described above. Failing to deliver instruction in such a manner, however, is to miss a key element of the data—the need to teach alphabetic principles and to do so directly and intensively and in a way that can virtually guarantee mastery. I would describe these practices as ongoing interventions that identify problems immediately and take immediate steps to remedy them before any deficits can accumulate.

If such intensive oversight is what is necessary to ensure early-level proficiency, why is it normally not carried out to such a degree in classrooms today? I have expounded on the reasons to some extent already, but, mainly, it is because the reading community is averse to such practices. It believes they cannot work and, in fact, might even be harmful to literacy attainment, in spite of all the empirical evidence that indicates otherwise.

As a result, attitudes toward a program like *Reading Mastery* can run the gamut. Some will automatically reject it on the basis of their previous training. Others might be concerned that adopting such methods will stigmatize them among their peers. Still others take issue with the need for a script, viewing such a tactic as presumptive of their inability to create effective lessons on their own. This loss of curricular autonomy also creates discomfort among many who are not accustomed to the kind of administrative oversight needed to maintain strict adherence to program fidelity. Some, especially experienced teachers who have never had to face such critical introspection, are downright outraged when told they must improve upon or modify their lesson delivery.

On the other hand, many others are more than happy to try something that purports to bring about the kind of success that has eluded them for so long. They are also happy to learn that the script relieves some of the burden of lesson planning. That comes as good news in a day and age when the focus of teacher evaluation is more about building achievement than simply maintaining order and creating environments akin to *Mister Rogers' Neighborhood*.

This is not meant to be sarcastic. Safe, warm, nurturing classrooms are essential to learning, and it takes skill and dedication to create and maintain them. But many teachers are beginning to recognize that highly structured reading lessons need not compromise their efforts in that regard, especially since the need for such regimentation is required for only a fraction of the school day. In addition, most educators realize that no other single factor is as important to a positive school climate as the esteem that results from actual achievement. And so, as difficult as it might be for some to modify their reading practices, many are beginning to find that there are compelling reasons to do so.[3]

NOTES

1. My reference to *Reading Mastery* is not meant as a sales pitch for a particular reading program. I have never worked for nor derived any compensation from its publisher or parent company. (Please see the section titled Resources for Teachers and Parents for a list of other research-based programs.)

2. Schaefer, *Creating World Class Schools: Peak Performance through Direct Instruction*, Presentation Notebook, 26–30.

3. The preceding chapter was completed with the help and collaboration of Doris Bisek, noted *Reading Mastery* practitioner, trainer, and consultant.

11

❦

Through Johnny's Eyes

"The poor in Resurrection City have come to Washington to show that the poor in America are sick, dirty, disorganized, and powerless—and they are criticized daily for being sick, dirty, disorganized, and powerless."

—Calvin Marshall

In 2009 the government changed its policy that had barred journalists from photographing the flag-draped coffins of combat victims. The premise behind this decision by the Obama administration was that, if we were forced to confront the realities of war, we would not be as inclined to engage in it unless we had taken the time and expended the energy to explore all other viable options. We would be even less motivated to expose our troops to the dangers of war if the entire country were required to look into the eyes of grief-stricken wives, children, and parents or visit hospital wards where double amputees were being fitted with prosthetic limbs and trying to figure out how to carry on with their lives.

The manner in which we choose to confront the harsh realities of reading failure should be put to that same kind of test. Perhaps then we might be more willing to look at options other than those that have failed Johnny for so long and so profoundly. Oh, I realize the issue is out there. We talk endlessly about it, and we try to assign blame in response to the reality of its existence. But most of us are never required to live it.

Consider the prospects of Johnny and other less fortunate individuals even prior to exiting the womb. They have a higher predisposition to experience traumas such as low birth weight, anoxia, fetal alcohol

119

syndrome, cocaine addiction, and other afflictions that will have serious repercussions on their physical, social, and cognitive development. Family stability is likely to be an issue, since low-income families are inclined to be headed by just one parent, often a mother who may not have reached adulthood herself. The presence of a father figure to provide financial assistance, or contribute in any meaningful way, is only a remote possibility.

In such families, finding the economic resources necessary to subsist is the parent's primary concern, making it more difficult to create an environment conducive to literacy development and the kind of language and prereading experiences middle-class families take for granted. The number of books, magazines, and newspapers in the home is significantly fewer than for those living in more privileged circumstances. And perhaps of even greater significance is the dearth of human interaction, as mothers are forced to work one or more jobs to make ends meet. All this happens during a critical period, one that serves as a precursor to literacy attainment. As a consequence, impoverished kids are likely to have amassed a literacy gap of years prior to ever setting foot in a classroom.

THE 30 MILLION WORD GAP

Betty Hart and Todd Risley analyzed the extent of these "developmental trajectories." In a two-and-a-half-year longitudinal study, they sought to "discover what was happening in children's early experience that could account for the wide discrepancy in rates of vocabulary growth that existed among four-year-olds."[1] They looked at three separate groups: children of professional families, children of working-class families, and children who participated in family assistance programs, an indication of their low socioeconomic status (SES). The data showed that "ordinary families differ immensely in the amount of experience with language and interaction they regularly provide their children."[2]

Table 11.1 depicts this inequity over a four-year time period.

The study revealed that poor children have only half the number of language interactions as children from working-class families and a whopping seventy-one percent fewer than children from professional backgrounds. But it's only the beginning.

These preexisting deficits require emergency attention. They must be not just prevented from widening even further; they must be removed entirely. Failure to do so will likely be disastrous. This is a documented fact too many educators seem to avoid. Dr. George Farkas, professor of social demography and education at Penn State University, suggests you can look at pretty much any grade and determine that those who are reading below level will continue to do so in succeeding years.[3]

Table 11.1. Number of Words of Language Experience

Families	One Week	One Year	Four Years
Professional	215,000	11,200,000	45,000,000
Working Class	125,000	6,500,000	26,000,000
Low SES	62,000	3,200,000	13,000,000

Source: Adapted from Hart and Risley, "The Early Catastrophe: The 30 Million Word Gap by Age 3," *American Educator,* Spring 2003, online, 5.

James Wendorf, executive director of the National Center for Learning Disabilities, puts it bluntly: "Reading is the gateway skill. It leads to all sorts of success, both academically and in life. It is the skill that undergirds most of the curriculum, and if children aren't learning that skill by the end of third grade, they are in desperate trouble."[4]

For far too long, our response to this disastrous predicament has been to take a laissez-faire approach, waiting around for Johnny to show an interest while immersing him in print resources. At some point, it is assumed he will suddenly kick into high gear and those debilitating deficits will magically vanish. But proceeding in such a fashion is to use Johnny as human capital by subjecting his literacy future to the vagaries of a crapshoot. Remember, it's not those who fail to make him a reader who stand to lose or suffer the most pain. It's Johnny himself. So let's consider the consequences if our gamble on his behalf fails to pay off. Let's look at it through Johnny's eyes.

THROUGH JOHNNY'S EYES

Kindergarten

Kindergarten is likely to be an enjoyable experience for Johnny. The day begins with a calendar activity in which the teacher points to the current date and reviews the days of the week and the months of the year. Later, Johnny gets to play with plenty of toys, visit the many interest centers, and interact with his classmates on the playground. Print material is in abundance. Johnny has several opportunities to leaf through books on his own, and, each day, the teacher reads several stories to the class.

Johnny also spends a lot of time learning to discriminate between numbers and shapes, and developing fine and gross motor skills through coloring, drawing, cutting, pasting, and enjoying the playground apparatus. He also works to identify letters of the alphabet and to recognize initial consonants in words. Most of this is done in a milieu of arts and crafts, coloring letters and numbers, cutting and pasting pictures that begin with a particular letter, collecting sets of objects, etc. However, systematized reading lessons are not included in Johnny's daily activities since they are not nearly as enjoyable and entertaining and might well discourage him from engaging in other reading endeavors. Better to surround him with books and to nurture and encourage his literacy progression. Given such an atmosphere, Johnny will learn to read just as naturally as he learned to speak. Won't he?

But it doesn't quite work that way for Johnny, and he leaves kindergarten unable to read more than a few words on his own. However, no alarm bells are ringing because reading readiness is all that is expected at this level. Actual reading ability lies somewhere down the road. Pushing Johnny to read any earlier is considered counterproductive because it is likely to destroy his motivation and prevent him from developing a love of reading for its own sake. And so Johnny enters first grade at a readiness level, a level in perfect alignment with what is developmentally appropriate.

First Grade

But is it really? Entering first grade at a readiness level means that, in the course of one hundred and eighty days, Johnny must somehow find a way to master the preprimer, primer, and first-grade material. He must do that if he is to read like a second grader at the end of the year. That is extremely unlikely since Johnny has received no systematic training in the alphabetic principle and, therefore, has little ability to decode words independently except those he has been able to remember. If he is going to recognize any other words, he must rely on other strategies such as context and/or picture clues. If those don't work, he can always ask someone else to pronounce unfamiliar words for him and, hopefully, remember when he encounters them in the future. Or he can simply guess in the hope that guessing wrongly doesn't cause him to misinterpret the textual message.

During his year in first grade, Johnny and his peers work their way through the basal reading book—which may contain some phonics—but hardly the kind of systematic treatment the research recommends. By midyear, he begins to lag behind many of his classmates, but the teacher refrains from placing him in a group with other below-level performers since this is likely to stigmatize him and cause him to suffer a loss of esteem. Johnny does make some progress, but is nowhere close to reading like a second grader by year's end.

Elementary School Continues

Johnny continues to struggle during second grade as his reading deficit becomes more significant. Shared reading periods become a humiliating experience as he gropes painstakingly through each and every word, succeeding with a few, requiring assistance with many others. More capable readers try to help by whispering the words or pronouncing them out loud, a phenomenon that exposes his handicaps to all and drives the reality of his inferiority ever more deeply into his consciousness. When he is called upon to read, other members of the class groan. The teacher seizes upon any opportunity to reinforce his efforts, but it becomes increasingly difficult to find such occasions and she begins calling on him less frequently.

For Johnny, school is no longer the joyful place it once had been. His writing ability reflects his rudimentary reading skills, and he cannot decode or comprehend most of the content in his science and social studies textbooks. His report card shows unsatisfactory progress in virtually all areas. He also gets low grades for social and emotional growth, which is characteristic of poor readers who seek to repress their anxiety and sense of inadequacy by becoming more aggressive with peers and more disruptive in the classroom. Given the choice between appearing dull or unruly, he quickly opts for the latter.

The teacher will do her best to discourage these behaviors and reinforce the positive, but, ultimately, she must mete out consequences. This causes Johnny to react with increasing resentment as the punishments and losses of privileges continue to pile up. Midway through the year, he begins receiving suspensions, his teacher having exhausted her repertoire of strategies to gain compliance. Staff and administration are all at wit's end about how to deal with Johnny, but he suffers as much as anyone. He gets less encouragement from adults, and he somehow knows that any praise he does receive is superficial and contrived.

Staff can't help but look to Johnny when there is trouble, and often they are right. Feelings of anger, shame, resentment, and inadequacy begin to overwhelm him, and he begins to suffer from a persecution complex since everyone seems to be ganging up on him. At times, he will respond to interventions, but he cannot escape the reality of his failures and any signs of acceptable school adjustment are short-lived.

New Schools

One day, Johnny comes home to find that he and his family have been evicted from their apartment. This is bad news, but Johnny is hardly disappointed at the prospect of attending a different school. The new school immediately diagnoses his reading shortcomings and responds by placing him in a small group, several members of which have been diagnosed as learning disabled. Johnny doesn't seem to mind all that much and actually responds enthusiastically because, for the first time, he can perform on a par with others. The small group intervention helps, and Johnny takes pride in the fact that there are now some books he can actually read on his own. He still lags behind and he is certainly no angel in the classroom, but his school adjustment has definitely taken a turn for the better.

During the summer, Johnny's mother gives birth to her fifth child. She seeks help from his grandmother, who agrees to have him live with her until Mom can get a bigger place. She tries to secure busing so he can continue at his current school, but the district is cash-strapped and unable to provide transportation. This will be Johnny's third school in four years, and there is little continuity with the previous school's program that would allow him to pick up where he left off. His recent progress comes to a screeching halt and the problem behaviors return.

Several months of dealing with Johnny's low performance and intransigent conduct prompt his teacher to suspect that Johnny has a learning disability, so he refers him for special programming. Mom is hesitant to sign off on the referral, refusing to believe there is anything wrong with him, viewing the idea of learning disability as some sort of mental defect. The diagnostic teacher tries to set her straight, but Mom is not buying it. However, when a parent advocate tells her that placement in a special program will restrict the school's ability to suspend him, she reluctantly gives her approval. The special education team, however, cannot document enough of a gap to warrant services. He's clearly behind, just not behind enough, and so he returns to the regular classroom.

Johnny's teacher would like to retain him in third grade but realizes that doing so will diminish his chances for special programming in the future. Promoting him means that the wide disparity between his grade level and his reading level that failed to qualify him previously could possibly double, bolstering his chances to meet criteria the following year. But the matter becomes moot when, in fourth grade, Johnny's mother is arrested for drug trafficking. Grandma is now on dialysis and no longer in a position to help. Johnny and his siblings are placed in foster care. Over the next three years, he lives with seven different families, and attends another three schools. If he truly does have a learning disability, he is unlikely to be placed anytime soon, since his school mobility strains the system's ability to monitor his progress.

Middle School and Beyond

For those next three years, Johnny never advances beyond a basic reading level. Each succeeding grade poses increasing cognitive challenges. The textbooks become more complex and require prior knowledge and skills far beyond his level of functioning.

He does continue to attend school regularly through most of his middle-school years, compiling a grade point average of just under 1.0. But when he enters high school, he begins to skip school on a regular basis, finding the streets preferable to attending classes he has little hope of passing. On a few occasions, he is detained by truancy officers who take him to a juvenile detention center and later release him to the custody of an aunt, his mother having been placed in a halfway house for recovering addicts.

Even though the aunt has legal custody, Johnny rarely spends his nights there. Most of the time he sleeps at friends' houses and apartments, crashing wherever it is most convenient. By age fifteen, he quits going to school entirely. His violent nature and willingness to break the law cause local gang leaders to aggressively recruit him, and he willingly accepts their overtures. He is fully aware of the dangers that accompany the affiliation, but in his mind the increased status and sense of belonging he has lacked for so long make it all worthwhile. That same year, he gets arrested for auto theft and possession of illicit drugs, and serves some time in another juvenile facility. Authorities assign him a school upon his release, but he is unlikely to show up more than one day a week. The streets remain a more viable option, and he supports himself with minimum wage jobs and some drug trafficking. He scarcely ever sees his family and, by the time he is nineteen, he has a long rap sheet. When he is caught in an armed robbery attempt, a judge sentences him to ten years in a state correctional institution.

SOMETIMES YOU JUST WANT TO CRY

The following excerpts are taken from the *Children of the Code* video.[5] All five students appear to be in their early to mid-teens. The names used are fictitious, but they are all real people who are now old enough to realize the impact their reading failure is having on their lives. Their words reflect a gamut of emotions including despair, anger, defiance, and fear.

You know sometimes you just want to cry. I mean why do you have to bother everybody else to be able to do things. And nobody knows how you feel unless they're in your shoes. That is really frustrating.

—Amanda

I struggle with reading. And like if I mess up or if I feel like I'm about to get messed up, I'll start to cry. I'll get angry. I'll just get mad at everybody, at the world, just because I don't know how to read.

—Adriana

I was in the third grade and I wasn't able to read since, and then, I was thinking—maybe it'll come along, it's gonna come along, but then it didn't. And then I started skipping class, saying "I'll learn how to read tomorrow, I'll learn how to read within the next week" and then pretty soon I kept putting it off and then that's when I became ashamed about not knowing how to read because there'd be kids younger than me that could read a book in no time and it'd take me two to three weeks just to read the same book.

—James

Like, the teacher would ask me to read something and I would read it and I'd get a wrong word or I'd go too slow and they'd make fun of me. I felt like beating the crap out of 'em.

—Robert

Well, one day we . . . well we had to go like in a circle and read and all that. I had a straw and a piece of paper, like a spit wad, and I threw a spit wad at the teacher. I got in trouble and I didn't have to read any more and I went, "Good. I don't have to read no more."

—Stephen

These videos can be viewed at www.childrenofthecode.org/Tour/c1/index.htm using the links "Social Danger," "Emotional Danger," "Academic Danger," and "Reading Matters."

A PATH TO HOPE

Obviously not everyone who struggles with reading will grow up to be a career criminal. And even if this Johnny had managed to become a proficient reader, and done so on an age-appropriate timeline, what is to say that he would not have followed that same tragic path? This Johnny had so many things working against him from the time he was born and throughout his life that reading ability alone guaranteed him nothing. But at least it would have given him a chance for a normal life. However, Johnny never got that chance, so people say that he failed. But exactly who failed whom?

Certainly students have a responsibility to take advantage of what schools offer, but schools must offer something of benefit. We are constantly reminded that reading programs should address individual needs. But exactly how individualized have we been when our so-called child-centric practices continue to fail so many? We did right by a good share of individuals, but whatever worked for them has been a dismal failure for others. Our response has been to thrust all the blame upon the families who suffer from such circumstances and, thereby, persecute them all the more. It is as if society has determined that children choose to be illiterate and that their parents are disinclined to do anything about it.

My experience tells me otherwise. We might choose to blame Johnny's mother and/or father but, don't forget, they most likely were born under the same circumstances as was he and, as such, faced the same impediments to literacy. As difficult as it might be for some to accept, the fact is that Johnny's mother loved him and wanted him to succeed as much as any parent anywhere.

We want parents to be accountable, but what about ourselves? It is easy to point to all the things we have done, all the interventions, and all the selfless acts on his behalf. But have we really looked beyond what we have always done for so long? Have we explored other areas and found places we never even knew existed? Have we questioned the narrow purview of training that chooses to omit some critical information? If we were to do this, we might discover some new truths.

We very well might find that we can do a lot more than provide a print-rich environment. We can even aspire beyond showing the likelihood that children will read on level. We can literally get to the point of guaranteeing it. You read that correctly. *Guarantee* it. No acceptance whatsoever that any of our children will ever pass through our doors without the literacy ability necessary to compete in a global society, the literacy to which everyone has a right, and which we are required to provide.

In order to make that happen, we will need to embrace some ideas we have scorned in the past and reject a few others we have always held dear.

First, we must dispel the notion that reading ability will occur in the normal progression of human development. We can no longer leave matters to chance by merely providing the best environment and greatest amount of nurturing.

We must be willing to cede the point that a hierarchy of skills that leads to literacy attainment does indeed exist and that it is our job to see to it that each and every single one of our students master each and every single one of those skills. In order for that to happen, we must follow specified procedures, the efficacy of which has been identified through scientific inquiry and then tested in classrooms.

We must come to terms with the fact that this may not always be fun and games, either for Johnny or his teacher. In carrying this out, we must not be fearful that Johnny will somehow be scarred or that his motivation will be destroyed. To the contrary, we need to proceed with confidence borne of knowing we will have given him the kind of mental discipline that will serve him well in countless other situations.

Educational leaders across the country will need to find ways to assure that these practices will become standard operating procedure so that, no matter what school Johnny attends and regardless of which community he finds himself, his journey toward literacy will never be interrupted.

If we have the collective will to do all these things, Johnny can go infinitely beyond learning to read and concentrate for the rest of his life on reading to learn. We owe this to Johnny. To think that we would ever do otherwise is beyond comprehension.

FELTUS TAYLOR

Things might have been different for Feltus Taylor. Of course, there could be no guarantees given that his prospects were bleak even while he lay in utero, waiting abandonment by his birth mother and abuse by his adoptive parents. Still, perhaps he might not have become such a violent person had he managed to attain even an ounce of esteem while growing up. But he lost that opportunity early on when the reality of his school failure was rudely chiseled into his being, destined to remain there right up to the day of his execution by the state of Louisiana.

While on death row he described to a case-worker, Dr. Cecile Guin, a researcher at Louisiana State University's school of social work, a day in second grade when his teacher had called him to the front of the room to write an answer next to a question she had inscribed on the chalkboard. He recounted standing there, immobilized by the fact that he could not read the question, much less write anything decipherable in response to it. He described to Dr. Guin the shame he experienced, the sensation of heat that overwhelmed his face and pulsated through his head, the utter humiliation he felt as he passed his classmates on the way back to his desk. To the very end, that was his most vivid recollection of all his years in school.

Still it is hard to shed any tears for a person who murdered a former co-worker with five shots to her head and upper body, and who later on that same day pumped another round into his former boss, permanently disabling him. The debate surrounding capital punishment notwithstanding, none would argue that Feltus owed a huge debt to society.

Dr. Guin notes that low literacy and overall school failure are common elements among nearly all her clients. What stymies her the most is the fact that most of them, including Feltus, are able to earn high school equivalency degrees while in prison. Why, she wonders, can't skills that hold the key to a normal productive life be attained early enough to avoid the prison experience entirely? And as to Feltus, she can only speculate whether both he and his victims might still be with us today had he possessed the ability that would have allowed him to avoid that painful experience in second grade.

NOTES

1. Hart and Risley, "The Early Catastrophe: The 30 Million Word Gap by Age 3," *American Educator*, Spring 2003, online, 2.

2. Hart and Risley, "The Early Catastrophe: The 30 Million Word Gap by Age 3," 2.

3. Farkas, *Children of the Code*, author's transcription from video.

4. Wendorf, interview, *Children of the Code*, www.childrenofthecode.org/tour/c1/index.htm.

5. Excerpts from *Children of the Code*, author's transcription from video, www.childrenofthecode.org/tour/c1/index.htm.

12

✒

Rescuing Johnny

"We have a stake in one another . . . what binds us together is greater than what drives us apart and . . . if enough people believe in the truth of that proposition and act on it, then we might not solve every problem, but we can get something meaningful done for the people with whom we share this earth."

—Barack Obama

I have put together a narrative that attempts to make sense of the disconnect between the literacy training Johnny has needed for so long and what he has received, but, in that, I surely have failed. For how can anyone make sense of a situation in which everyone claims to have the same goal, but is nevertheless unwilling to look beyond what has failed to accomplish it? How can one explain the obstinacy of some who reject outright anything that doesn't reflect their narrowly defined versions of the truth? How can one account for this when there is so much more to accommodate than to disdain?

What is it that causes us to operate all over the pedagogical map, to proceed in hit or miss fashion, the rationale being that good people will do good things and, thereby, good results are bound to occur? We would not tolerate that kind of behavior in other professions. When we visit a doctor, we expect her to minister to us based on known remedies and treatments rather than what she values or believes. How might we react if she advised us to immerse ourselves in a healthy environment and think positive thoughts and eventually we will get well? Her malpractice insurance premium is a testament to how little slack we give her in that regard.

But it appears that schools and districts and teacher preparation institutions have a license to do much as they please, and not have cause to worry when things go terribly wrong. The result is a form of goal displacement, a condition in which the ultimate goal is replaced by something else. We see this kind of thing happen, for example, when churches resort to festivals featuring gambling and alcohol. The goal of sustaining the organization begins to take precedence over the message it aspires to convey to its members.

In reading education, protecting one's professional turf seems to have eclipsed the ultimate purpose of making everyone a reader. My explorations cause me to conclude that the holistic movement has proven to be the more intransigent voice, far more unwilling to accommodate divergent perspectives than their code-based counterparts.

That is not to say that code-based proponents have not contributed to the discord. Yes, there are phonics lobbies out there, and, yes, they do in many instances attack the various expressions of holism. And, yes, they can get quite mean-spirited at times, which I will admit doesn't help. But their ultimate goal has not been to squelch everything other than phonics. Rather, they are merely seeking to assure that their children will have this fundamental tool for literacy. They would have little to complain about if, when their youngsters read to them at home, they showed some facility to sound out an unfamiliar word. Oftentimes when they express bewilderment over their children's inability to demonstrate this skill, they are made to feel as though they were misguided or unenlightened.

RESCUING JOHNNY

Three years ago, I began an arduous journey into the world of early reading and emerged with a somewhat revised perspective, one that prompts me to ask a few questions and to challenge the educational establishment to some degree. I realize that my perspective is just one among many and that I would be as cavalier as those I have criticized if I were to suggest that I had all of the answers. I certainly don't. But there is one matter about which I am certain, that having to do with coalition building. Johnny is imploring us to work together. And the only way that can happen is for those on both sides of the debate to expand their viewpoints so as to accommodate all that has been learned. But, as we have seen, that kind of unification is not something we in education have eagerly pursued. Still it is a worthy goal in my opinion, but one that cries out for answers if we are ever to meet it.

CAN WE CHANGE OUR ATTITUDE?

Oftentimes we have seen how a fundamental shift in viewpoints can improve health and safety and overall quality of life. Remember when every table in every restaurant had an ashtray right next to the ketchup? Recall the time when adult smokers had no need to huddle furtively outside in the elements looking like gangsters planning their next heist? Go back to those days when few cars had seat belts and most chose not to use them, even when they became standard equipment in all automobiles. It wasn't that long ago when we would see children climbing over seat backs, hanging out windows, and nesting on the shelf just below the rear window. But today, we would never even think about simply throwing our kids in the car and going on our merry way.

Those things don't happen today because our attitudes about health and safety have changed dramatically, driven by realities revealed to us through testing, experimentation, and statistical analysis. Those tools exposed the relationship between smoking and disease and made us mindful of what we needed to do to protect ourselves and our children while traveling in motor vehicles. Society has come full circle in response to those issues. Might not reading science be able to benefit in a similar manner?

Right now, things like systematic phonics, directed teaching, and intensive curricular treatment are viewed as passé, anti-child-centric, and anti-meaning-based. Do we really need to perceive these constructs in such a fashion? Might there be a way to accommodate the phonics message and still be child-centric? Is there a path that would lead us to see code-based training in an entirely differently light? Might that happen to the extent that no self-respecting school would ever even think of using a reading program that didn't guarantee all of its children the ability to decode words independently?

CAN WE BE ACCOUNTABLE?

Our failure to deal with reality, our unwillingness to cooperate with one another and to get down off our pedagogical towers, has left us in a state of suspended stagnation. Whether we can mount an offensive, galvanize around the ultimate goal, and challenge those who would interfere remains to be seen. A lot will depend on how deeply we are willing to look inside ourselves.

- Are we willing to admit we have a serious problem?
- Are we willing to admit that our own failures, in large measure, have caused and sustained the problem?

- Are we willing to modify our own behavior, even when it means doing things we would never have thought to do in the past, things that are difficult, and things we would prefer not to do?
- Are we willing to resist peer pressure, to separate politics and ideology, and never lose sight of what it is exactly that we seek to accomplish?

We can do all these things if we choose to. We can choose to lose weight, stop smoking, and limit our salt and sugar intake because the *research makes it clear that we can extend and improve the quality of our lives by doing so.* And we can also choose to teach phonics to children at the earliest of levels in a direct and intensive fashion *because the research makes it clear that we can improve the quality of children's learning and the quality of their lives by doing so.*

WHY NOT ADDRESS READING FAILURE AS THE PUBLIC HEALTH CRISIS IT TRULY IS?

We have heard many alerts and many alarms about the consequences of illiteracy and low literacy, but we haven't seen the kind of response to them that we see with other issues. Look at what happens when, say, *The New England Journal of Medicine* publishes just one study that suggests a link between anti-inflammatory drugs and increased risk of heart disease. The public is subjected to a media blitz. Doctors, pharmacists, and medical health professionals throughout the country are warned. The drug company's stock plummets, and class action attorneys swoop in like rabid dogs. Society shows its immediate and collective will to prevent even one more individual from being victimized.

The reading crisis gets no such intense reaction. We tolerate a condition that has as much or more of an impact on the safety and well-being of children and society as do risky pharmaceuticals. Perhaps such urgency is lacking because the impact of reading failure on any given individual is not immediately discernible. It's like a child born with a congenital heart defect. It may not be life-threatening at first, but will ultimately become so. However, if doctors can recognize the condition early, they are in a position to do something before it is too late. Why wouldn't we take that same approach with reading? What's to prevent us from treating children's preexisting deficits much as we do a disease, immediately and based on the strongest of experimental and clinical evidence?

CAN READING SCIENCE DRIVE
EDUCATIONAL DECISION-MAKING?

There was a time when reading science was fuzzy, incoherent, diffuse, and based on rudimentary research practices. But that time is long since past. Social scientists have learned how to develop and apply ever more sophisticated techniques to overcome those challenges that are specific to their disciplines. Each generation of research has improved upon that of its predecessors and the aggregate data leave little to the imagination.

School boards, school administrations, and educational agencies should have the ability to factor empirical evidence into their decision-making processes. To guide them in that endeavor, they must know which programs have passed experimental muster and which have not. Right now that is difficult because we do not require publishers to specify that on their product. That is unfortunate, given that other commodities that purport to affect one's health and well-being must follow rigid guidelines in that regard.

I found the following statement on the bottle of a dietary supplement: "May reduce coronary heart disease risk." However, on the back, in much smaller print, there were these messages regarding the claim on the front: "This statement has not been evaluated by the Food and Drug Administration," and, "This product is not intended to diagnose, treat, cure or prevent any disease."

Educational decision makers should have that same benefit to guide them when selecting reading materials. A couple suggestions: "Warning: There is no clinical evidence attesting to the effectiveness of this reading program." We might also want to alert textbook adoption committees to the presence of negative correlations: "This reading program has been found to produce reading failure in a representative sampling of school-age children."

This may sound tongue-in-cheek, but it's not meant to be. There's nothing funny about reading programs that don't deliver on their promises. And don't we owe, to those who make critical decisions on our children's behalf, the benefit of that knowledge when it exists?

DO WE HAVE THE COLLECTIVE WILL TO GUARANTEE
ALPHABETIC MASTERY TO ALL CHILDREN?

Consider the comments of Robert W. Sweet, Jr., president and co-founder of The National Right to Read Foundation:

> Historically, all American school children were taught to read. Teachers never considered that a child "could not" be taught to read and remedial reading was unheard of. In fact, the first remedial reading clinic opened in

1930, soon after the results of the "look and say" (the so-called "Dick and Jane" program) reading methods were beginning to be felt.

Up until the early part of the 20th century, children were taught to read by first learning the alphabet, then the sounds of each letter, how they blended into syllables, and how those syllables made up words. They were taught that English spelling is logical and systematic, and that to become a fluent reader it was necessary to master the alphabetic "code" in which English words are written to the point where it (the code) is used automatically with little conscious thought given to it.

Once a child learned the mechanics of the code, attention could be turned to more advanced content.[1]

In other words, there was a time when teaching reading and teaching the alphabetic code were one and the same, a system that yielded some pretty impressive results. In fact, the National Assessment of Adult Literacy reports that, between 1870 and 1940, the illiteracy rate plummeted from 20 percent of the overall population to a mere 2.9 percent. During that same period, illiteracy among blacks fell from 79.9 percent to 11.5 percent.[2] Many concluded that the scourge of illiteracy might soon be eradicated.

It would seem that, if reading instruction were going to remain the purview of the schools, it would be in everyone's best interest for them to galvanize around the code-based message. At least they could say that, if they didn't do anything else for Johnny, they will have bestowed upon him knowledge that provides the surest path to literacy.

The fact that this doesn't happen in the regular course of school training prompts one to ask several questions. Why would we abandon, or give only cursory treatment to, alphabetic training of an alphabetic language? Why would we turn a deaf ear to parents who have always valued this kind of instruction for their children? Why would we deny them the sheer delight and utter satisfaction that comes from seeing their offspring begin decoding words on their own? Why would we ignore decades of empirical evidence that screams out on behalf of those same parents? And why is it necessary for some parents to throw their hands up in utter frustration and take it upon themselves to do for their children what the schools cannot or will not, as was the case with Mona McNee?

JUST PLAIN MRS. MONA MCNEE

The reading wars are not limited to the United States alone. Indeed, I found similar versions in other English-speaking countries including Great Britain, Australia, and New Zealand. Nowhere is this better exemplified than with the case of eighty-six-year-old Mona

McNee, a retired teacher residing in Merseyside, an area along the River Mersey in the northwest of England. I came to know Mona through a blog that deals with reading and reading disabilities. She began one of her posts to me with the following:

> I am just plain Mrs. Mona McNee M.B.E. (Member of the Order of the British Empire). I got this honour (for "Services to Education") with the Queen's birthday this past summer.
>   I was a teacher of geography in a grammar (secondary in Britain) school, and had a Down's Syndrome son (mosaic I now believe). After two school years, he could read and spell three-letter words like run and six. Then the system moved him to an ESN (Educationally Subnormal) school with specially qualified teachers, and framed certificates on the wall![3]

Mona has a colorful way of describing her frustration with the reading establishment. The following is but one example:

> Then we have the extraordinary idea that children will more easily read a word they are interested in! It has long been held that it is important for teachers to realise that children will not be attracted to studying words unless they have been strongly motivated . . . words which appeal to them strongly and relate to their everyday experience. This is not scientific. And so much of what they "find" has come from looking at pupils denied the simple c-a-t introduction. A whole world of mythical theory has been developed, along with a massive establishment well paid, claiming to be well-intentioned and knowledgeable, that has kept common sense at bay for sixty years in England, longer in America. There was no need for all this "expertise." And it has persisted through decades of poor reading. Half the children in juvenile court are dyslexic. So . . . scapegoats provided, blame home, child, family, "poverty," environment. Never, never blame the teaching.[4]

However, Mona is not one to just complain. When her Down's Syndrome son's school could not teach him to read, she did it herself using a simple code-based program. While she never got a certificate to teach reading, she sees that as a good thing.

"I received my teaching diploma in 1947–8 or so, to teach geography. I have never had ANY (mis)training in how to teach reading—and that is why I never got it wrong. Others were FAR better than I at teaching children but I was FAR better than they at teaching reading!"[5]

She has continued working with individuals since her retirement from the schools in 1981, swamped by parents begging for help, and "by now has taught well over 500 dyslexics and other adults and children with reading difficulties." Because she was unable to accommodate all who requested her assistance, she developed and published *Step By Step: A Day-by-Day Programme of Systematic, Synthetic Phonics*. The program was first copyrighted in 1990, and is now in its sixth printing, the most recent in 2008.[6] (See Resources for Teachers and Parents for ordering information.)

The following passage about Mona's experience with her son is taken from *The Great Reading Disaster*. It was written by Alice Coleman, co-author of the book:

> Mona rediscovered the lost efficacy of phonics teaching when faced with the most challenging of tasks: introducing her Down's Syndrome son to the skills that eventually made him a fluent reader. Tim had been fortunate in his infant school, where he learned by the phonics method, relating letters to sounds. He was taught the sounds of the alphabet and by the age of seven, he could decipher and spell three-letter words such as "run" and "fox."
>
> He was then placed in an ESN (educationally sub-normal) school with specially qualified staff who should have been able to accelerate his learning, but actually brought it to a complete standstill. They regarded traditional phonics as politically incorrect and substituted the Progressivist system with its look-say reading methodology. This disregarded the sounds of letters and was based on the purely visual recognition of the appearance of words as wholes, which gave it the alternative name of the whole-word method. As Progressivism began, progress stopped. Tim stagnated on Ladybird Book 2 for two years but the teachers' message to Mona McNee remained, "Don't interfere. You will muddle him."
>
> For two long years she stood by, wondering why his good start had been followed by a failure to go on learning. Then she attended a parents' meeting and saw, on the classroom wall, something done by every child except her own. She talked to the teacher, a specialist with good discipline, but received no hope and went out to her car and sat and sobbed.
>
> "Well," she thought, "for all their qualifications they have taught him nothing and I can't do worse than that." She had never tried to teach anyone to read and did not even remember learning to read herself, but by the grace of God she came across the Royal Road Readers, which were phonics-based and introduced words in a graded order of difficulty. They were very good for children who already knew their letters and sounds. She started with Book 1, Part 1, page 1, and steadily plodded through the lot: exercises, stories, and companion books. She did not know if Tim would ever really learn and after reading Pearl Buck's account of her daughter's attempts, was ready to quit at any

time if he became distressed. All she knew was that he had not reached the limit of his potential and so she kept going.

Looking back now, when she teaches with a liberal use of games, she realises that Tim did it the hard way with no light relief. Every morning they worked for twenty minutes before school and continued through the holidays. In eighteen months, he reached the end of Book Nine and could read! At school he was still sitting with Ladybird Book 2 and she had to tell his teachers that he was literate. They tested him and found that it was true.

Now he reads whatever he wants: the Observer Aircraft book, the names of countries which he can find in the atlas, and words such as "reconnaissance," which he understands. He once asked what "skit" meant and as his mother began to explain, he said, "Oh, you mean parody." He can read a map to navigate on car trips and can find his own television programmes. Like many with reading problems, he sticks to non-fiction and is particularly interested in history. On the genealogical tree of the Royal Family, he would do well on Mastermind.

His life today would be very different if he had not learned to read. But Mona McNee asks herself, "Why, oh why, did I wait two years? I saw for myself that someone well able to learn was simply not being taught by his qualified teachers."[7]

Reprinted with permission, Imprint Academic, Exeter, UK

IS IT TIME TO EXPAND ON
WHAT IT MEANS TO BE CHILD-CENTRIC?

Of course we want to respect children's individuality, their interests, their learning styles, their creative instincts. And yes, we want school to be an enjoyable experience, one that fosters growth in all domains, whether cognitive, affective, or social. But is that to suggest that children should never have to struggle, never have the need to show resolve and perseverance when the solutions to problems don't just fall into their laps? And is it such a bad thing to devote some time toward building foundational skills that might not have immediate significance but will in the end prove to be of infinite value? Child-centrism is a laudable value, but it involves so much more than what we have previously assigned to it.

A child-centric curriculum bases instruction on empirical evidence.

Distinguished scientists have devoted their entire careers toward filling what had previously been a research gap. From there they have

proceeded to expand and improve upon those efforts in order to bring
the matter of early reading into ever-sharper focus. The research base is
so strong, and its findings have been replicated so often, that it is mind-
boggling that so many are willing to brush it off as though it had no merit
whatsoever. It is difficult to fathom that those who choose to ignore it, or
undermine it, or castigate it, could ever have the audacity to claim to be
using anything even remotely associated with the very notion of child-
centrism. It is literally akin to withholding food and water when such
commodities are in abundance.

A child-centric curriculum builds esteem based on performance rather than pretense.

All too often, educators are unwilling even to suggest to a child that he or
she is performing below level. We name reading groups after birds, and
we present students with meaningless certificates of achievement. We
even tiptoe around grades. Many children never see the letters A, B, C, D,
and F on their report cards. Instead of letter grades, they encounter words
like "emerging" or "progressing." Why not just level with Johnny and his
parents by telling them the truth in terms they can easily understand? I seriously doubt such unabashed candor will damage a kid forever, especially
when so many of our children are forced to deal with life circumstances that
impact on their emotional well-being to a far more significant degree.

We do a disservice to children by giving them a false perception of
where they stand on the literacy continuum. To be child-centric, therefore, is to be honest and straightforward, so that we do not give children
the notion that they are doing well when, in fact, they are not. If we truly
want to be respectful of them, then we need to exude confidence that they
can accept the truth and use it as motivation to achieve at higher levels.

A child-centric curriculum builds a strong work ethic.

Throughout my career, anything drill-based was considered as antithetical to the notion of child-centrism. "Drill and kill" was the operational
phrase, giving one the perception that such tactics would kill off a child's
motivation to read or engage meaningfully in classroom activities. We
have become entranced with the idea that every activity should involve
experiences that are at once joyful and amusing. We do this to such an
extent that language arts is better described as "literary arts and crafts."[8]

Or perhaps "language arts and crafts." As J. E. Stone noted,

> What . . . so many . . . experts are finding reflects an often disagreeable truth
> about learning: Learning takes study and study takes time and effort.

The idea that learning should be motivated solely by interest and enthusi-asm not only ignores the role of work, but also skews the focus of education.[9]

If parents, teachers, and, indeed, society as a whole want children to benefit fully from school, they must insist that students study and make an effort to learn whether they feel like it or not.

Certainly we are remiss if we expect children to engage in high-intensity, drill-based fashion throughout the day. But if we wish to honor children's lifelong needs, we need to let them know that, when it comes to achieving at high levels, the operational words are practice, practice, practice. And, yes, drill can and does aid in the process just like it does in so many other endeavors.

How can we expect children to develop this kind of discipline—the kind employers will insist upon or the kind that will set one worker apart from another—if we never put forth this expectation? Even the most gifted shortstop takes ground ball after ground ball in practice so that nearly every chance during a game appears as routine. Even the greatest piano virtuoso had need to plunk out repetitive scales to develop the au-tomaticity that would allow her or him to concentrate entirely on musical interpretation.

So what is so wrong with some intense instruction that leads to master-ing the sounds and symbols of an alphabetic language? Such procedures are far more likely to build, rather than undermine, motivation. The re-ward comes each time students put those phonemes together and realize they have sounded out a previously unfamiliar word and done it on their very own. And what better encouragement is there than the beaming faces of parents when their children read entire pages of text instead of having the pages read to them?

Shielding our kids from a little hard work for fear that they will some-how come to despise reading is an expression of disrespect to students and teachers alike. It disparages pupils because it implies that they are incapable of sustaining their focus long enough to be productive. And it is derisive of teachers because it assumes they lack the management skills necessary to keep children on task and to demonstrate equilibrium in their choice of classroom activities.

A child-centric curriculum teaches pupils at their current level of functioning.

We also demonstrate child-centrism when we teach students at their appropriate levels. Students have a right to receive—and educators a re-sponsibility to provide—instruction on a par with an individual student's ability to learn. The perception that ability grouping is inherently bad is both naïve and cruel. Would we expect first-year algebra students to proceed immediately to advanced calculus? How would a technologically challenged adult feel among a group of computer wizards in a software training session? If one's goal is to preserve a child's esteem, it makes no sense whatsoever to place him in a setting where he is incapable of meaningful participation and where his inferiority is on display for all to see.

A child-centric curriculum is impervious to politics and ideology.

If we are to put children at the center of our efforts, we have a responsibility to instruct them based on validly derived truths. Allowing politics or ideology to enter into the dialogue is to bury such truths. Should Muslims disregard the principles of immunology because a Christian discovered them? Should Democrats oppose No Child Left Behind because it was introduced by a Republican administration? My own politics notwithstanding, I just have a hard time condemning any effort that pursues measures than can offer a track record of success. It's not politics or religion that is at stake here. It's children and their futures.

It is depressing each day to read one negative comment after another, to hear about why something can't work, or how unfair something is, or how one side stands to gain at the expense of another. It is especially discouraging to hear so much nay-saying and so few calls for cooperation and meaningful action among stakeholders while children are left to struggle and fail.

HAVE OUR NOTIONS ABOUT READING READINESS AND DEVELOPMENTAL APPROPRIATENESS CONTRIBUTED TO READING DISABILITY?

For far too long we have been willing to accept reading readiness as the age-appropriate goal for children at the end of the kindergarten year. Perhaps Rudolph Flesch was right when he contended that this notion of readiness could well represent a deprivation of needed instruction during a critical period. It makes sense. Those who study human growth and development are familiar with the term "critical period." There are critical periods in the development of a fetus during which essential nutrients can penetrate the wall of the placenta. If the nutrients are present during this time, the organism will grow and prosper. Withholding these nutrients during this period can have long-term deleterious effects.

The toddler years represent a *critical period* for language acquisition. This includes learning to comprehend the spoken word, learning to speak, and, later, recognizing and interpreting symbolic application in text. Only in rare circumstances does a child come to school without some measure of speaking capability. But that doesn't necessarily lead to reading competency without direct intervention by a teacher or other adult. And that intervention must occur early because, by kindergarten, children are approaching the latter stages of that critical period in which text interpretation is best facilitated. Failing to intervene when necessary might well jeopardize the chance that it will ever occur. Children may not be clamoring for this kind of instructional treatment, but the need for it is present nonetheless.

Therefore, a strong case can be made that it would be developmentally inappropriate to deny children these kinds of direct and systematic interventions. The data certainly would bear that out. If one wants to observe developmental inappropriateness in its purest form, all one would need to do is to visit third grade classrooms where children are incapable of decoding even simple words. Follow those same individuals into the intermediate years and note how many read below even basic levels. But don't stop there. Visit the middle schools where grade point averages for many hover below 1.0, due mainly to their inability to read and comprehend the ever more sophisticated text in their schoolbooks. When we see such egregious examples of developmental inappropriateness at those levels, perhaps it would be a good idea to revisit what it means to a kid in kindergarten when he or she still has a chance to overcome so many obstacles to literacy.

WILL SCHOOLS OF EDUCATION JOIN IN THE EFFORT TO PROMOTE THE SCIENCE AND GIVE MORE EMPHASIS TO CODE-BASED TRAINING?

It is hard to fathom that those who sign off on teacher certification would choose to ignore the science that undergirds their profession. This is especially troubling when doing so would not necessitate that they abandon any of the measures that have guided their efforts for so long. As one noted researcher maintains:

> Universities have to dig much deeper in order to lead on this issue instead of follow, kicking and screaming under political pressure, to meet these challenges of teacher preparation. They have not done a good job.[10]

Doing a better job would include assurance that teacher candidates and those involved in ongoing professional development learn:

- the full range of the scientific enterprise regarding early reading
- the means whereby they can critically analyze and interpret the data
- the distinctions between the various research platforms, including the respective capabilities and limitations of each

- how to take advantage of the symbiotic relationship that exists between phonological and holistic practices

Apart from that, in this day and age of ever more stringent oversight and accountability, our teachers merit the kind of training that relates specifically to how they will be evaluated. And therefore, these same schools of education must incorporate into their methods classes:

- sequentially guided programs that, when successfully completed, guarantee on-level performance for all students by year's end
- strategies in which daily measures of pupil progress occur as a natural outgrowth of the lesson so as to keep to a minimum the need for formal testing
- daily intervention practices to guide students along a predetermined path to literacy acquisition

In order to bring this about, schools of education will need to modify their stance to some extent and come to terms with the data that indicate there is a hierarchy of skills that, when mastered, leads to reading competence. Without such a road map, there is absolutely no way to ascertain whether a student is making adequate progress, and reading pedagogy is relegated to a form of high-stakes gambling. It is unconscionable to think that the best way to make readers of all kids is to respect their individual timelines toward literacy and only worry about it later when the magic never happens. Our kids deserve better than that.

NOTES

1. Sweet, *Illiteracy: An Incurable Disease or Education Malpractice?*, www.nrrf.org/essay_Illiteracy.html.

2. Institute of Education Sciences, National Center for Education Statistics, *National Assessment of Adult Literacy*, nces.ed.gov/surveys/ALL/.

3. In a posting on groups.yahoo.com/group/readbygrade3/, July 19, 2008.

4. In a posting on groups.yahoo.com/group/readbygrade3/, June 10, 2008.

5. In an email dated February 18, 2009.

6. McNee, *Step By Step: A Day-by-Day Programme of Systematic, Synthetic Phonics for all Ages*, copyright 2008.

7. McNee and Coleman, *The Great Reading Disaster*, 8–9.

8. Calkins, quoted in Schmoker, "Radically Redefining Literacy Instruction," 492.

9. Stone, "Learning Requires More Than Play," 2.

10. Moats, *Children of the Code*, author's transcription from video.

Epilogue

Surely, between these extremes, there must be a medium not difficult to be found. And is not this the middle course, which all sensible and judicious men, all patriots, and all genuine republicans, must approve? . . .

Such being the rule . . ., it will come to be universally understood, that political proselytism is no function of the school; but that all indoctrination into matters of controversy between hostile political parties is to be elsewhere sought for, and elsewhere imparted. . . .

[A]nd thus, too, will that pernicious race of intolerant zealots, whose whole faith may be summed up in two articles,—that they, themselves, are always infallibly right, and that all dissenters are certainly wrong—be extinguished—extinguished, not by violence, nor by proscription, but by the more copious inflowing of the light of truth.[1]

The preceding words provide some valuable exhortations to the reading community, if it is to do right by Johnny and his cohorts. However, as the reader may have surmised, they were written not for the educators of today, but for those who plied their craft some one hundred and sixty years ago.

They are, in fact, the words of Horace Mann in his Twelfth (and last) Report to the Board of Education of the Commonwealth of Massachusetts and were written in 1848. There is some irony in that fact, given that today's school approach to reading is a full 180 degrees removed from that in Mann's day. But they ring true nonetheless, and it is difficult to argue with Mann when he puts forth the notions that:

- "Sensible" and "judicious" people can put aside their differences and find a middle ground about which they can unite.

145

- In order to find such middle ground, politics and ideology must be expunged from the general discourse.
- The "light of truth" must be used to expose those "intolerant zealots" who would interfere with this process.

So, where have we come in those one hundred and sixty years? How far have we advanced in the struggle to bring literacy ability to all in the republic? How "sensible and judicious" have we been, when the front pages of our daily newspapers and the Internet blogs are filled with the same kind of rancor and hostility that prompted Mann to write with such a vitriolic pen? Have we exorcised politics and ideology? Have we found a way to eradicate those who would seek to prevent the "light of truth" from penetrating our classroom walls?

Those are not meant to be rhetorical questions and, in fact, have very specific answers. Yes, we have identified a middle ground, but we have chosen not to implement it or, at least, not to the degree necessary to reap its full benefit. Politics and ideology are still front and center and play an enormous role in reading policy and decision making. And zealots continue to profess their infallibility and prevent the "light of [scientific] truth" from penetrating classroom walls. And, because of this, we continue to leave Johnny and his classmates cruelly—and needlessly—behind.

Many will criticize me for much, if not most, of what I have written. They will criticize me especially for taking sides, for embracing the research and casting as villains those who reject it. Such actions, they will probably maintain, do little to resolve anything and, in fact, fan the flames of an already raging firestorm of controversy.

But those who would berate me for embracing the science are oblivious to a fundamental truth and that is that *the research represents the middle ground*. What is conspicuous about its message is its lack of exclusivity, refusing to claim that any one method, be it code-based or meaning-based, in itself guarantees any child a passport to literacy. Those who would assail me for embracing the research message also ignore the fact that it is the product of "sensible and judicious" men and women, those to whom Mann was appealing to bring the "light of truth" to the rancorous debate.

So I am prepared to accept the onslaught of criticism that is sure to follow. But I wish to point out that I am just the messenger. If you assail me, you must also be willing to take aim at Jeanne Chall, the Harvard professor whose findings have withstood countless challenges and never been disproved. You must be willing to demean the efforts of Marilyn Adams, whose work is cited in virtually every major study that deals with reading and reading science. You must be willing to cast aside the resolute findings of the National Research Council, the Commission on

Reading, the National Reading Panel, and, most recently, the Report of the National Early Literacy Panel. These consortiums represent the work of hundreds of distinguished scholars who divorced themselves from the emotionalism surrounding their work and pursued with endless rigor the purest expression and implementation of the scientific method. You certainly have the right to believe and act contrary to their relentless efforts and unambiguous conclusions, and still profess to have put children first. But you must forgive me if I find that it is not "sensible and judicious" to do so.

Judge:	*The defendant is charged with Phonological Assault upon the nation's youth. What say you?*
Foreman:	*We're sorry, Your Honor. We have not reached a verdict. We are hopelessly deadlocked.*
Judge:	*These are serious charges. I must remind you that reaching a verdict isn't an option for you. It is a requirement. The literacy futures of children are at stake.*
Foreman:	*I realize that, Your Honor, but we cannot seem to agree as to whether or not the defendant judiciously carried out empirical evidence.*
Judge:	*But the evidence has been laid out. It is a matter of record.*
Foreman:	*I know, Your Honor. Some of us agree with the evidence but others do not. They don't believe in it.*
Judge:	*This is an outrage. Your verdict must reflect the evidence, not what you believe to be the evidence.*
Foreman:	*I tried to make that clear, Your Honor. But some of us refuse to budge.*
Judge:	*Well, I too refuse to budge. You are to return to the jury room and not show your faces again until you can render a verdict. I simply will not allow reasonable and judicious people to shirk their responsibility. We all await your final decision.*

NOTES

1. Cremin, ed., *The Republic and the School*, 97.

Acknowledgments

L *eaving Johnny Behind* spilled out of me because of my commitment to-ward children's literacy, a passion for making readers of all children, especially among those who began the process with the odds stacked against them. That passion would not have existed were it not for the example of those professional men and woman that surrounded me throughout my career, people who demonstrated their love and dedica-tion to children in countless ways, who never lost sight of the real reason they went to work every day. I would be remiss if I failed to acknowledge their relentless efforts.

First of all, to the staff at 21st St. School in Milwaukee, where I spent the majority of my career. These were indeed courageous people who were never intimidated by the challenge of marching each day into one of the most impoverished areas in the country and laying their collective souls on the line for those who needed them the most.

Thanks also to that core group of direct instruction principals in Mil-waukee, dynamic individuals with patience and fortitude and selfless resolve on behalf of children's reading advancement. Ours was a special bond, and I thank them for all they taught me about leadership and what it means to remain steadfast in pursuit of a common goal.

To my son, Nicholas Pedriana, and his wife, Teri Fritsma, both of them writers, researchers, and doctors of sociology. Through our lively discus-sions, they eventually taught me how to distinguish among the various research platforms, and thereby how to identify the ambiguities that keep legitimate data from gaining acceptance in classrooms.

To my friend, Robert Buege, successful author and noted baseball historian, who challenged me to do more than merely talk about a problem. Were it not for his advice, prodding, and encouragement, this book would probably never have gotten beyond the planning stages.

To my brother Tom, who lent his analysis and perspective on the early draft, valuable insight to say the least.

And perhaps more than anyone else, I owe a debt of gratitude to the parents, children, and grandchildren of the 21st St. School community. Their lives are interwoven throughout my being and my life has been enriched for having had the chance to work among, together, and on behalf of them all.

Resources for
Teachers and Parents

RESEARCH-BASED READING PROGRAMS

The programs listed below have been validated through quantitative/empirical research and are appropriate for use under the Response to Intervention model used to diagnose and remediate reading problems. Such programs include but are not limited to the following:

Alphabetic Phonics©
Contact   Nancy Coffman
Address   TSRH/LWCDC
          2222 Wellborn
          Dallas, TX 75219
Website   http://ALTAread.org
Phone   214-559-7800

Association Method©
Contact   Maureen Martin
Address   USM Dubard SLD
          188 College Drive #10035
          Hattiesburg, MS 39406
Website   http://usm.edu/dubard
Phone   601-266-5223

Corrective Reading©
Contact   Customer Service
           SRA McGraw-Hill
Address   220 East Danieldale Road
           DeSoto, TX 75115
Website   http://SRAonline.com
Phone   888-772-4543

Fundations©
Contact   Wilson Language Training
Address   47 Old Webster Road
           Oxford, MA 01540
Website   http://www.wilsonlanguage.com
Phone   800-899-8454

Horizons©
Contact   Customer Service
           SRA McGraw-Hill
Address   220 East Danieldale Road
           DeSoto, TX 75115
Website   http://SRAonline.com
Phone   888-772-4543

Just Words©
Contact   Wilson Language Training
Address   47 Old Webster Road
           Oxford, MA 01540
Website   http://www.wilsonlanguage.com
Phone   800-899-8454

Language!©
Contact   S. Ashmore
           Sopris West
Address   4093 Specialty Place
           Longmont, CO 80504
Website   http://SoprisWest.com
Phone   800-547-6747

Lindamood-Bel©
Contact   Paul Worthington
           Lindamood Bell
Address   416 Higuera Street
           San Luis Obispo, CA 93401

Website   http://Lindamoodbell.com
Phone   805-541-3836

A Legacy of Literacy©
Contact   Customer Service
          Houghton Mifflin
Address   9205 Southpark Center Loop
          Orlando, FL 32819
Website   http://www.hmhschool.com
Phone   800-225-5425

Lexia Learning Systems©
Contact   Customer Support
          Lexia Learning Systems
Address   200 Baker Avenue
          Concord, MA 01742
Website   http://www.lexialearning.com/products/index.php
Phone   800-435-3942 Ext. 231

Orton-Gillingham
Contact   Priscilla Hoffman
Address   AOGPE
          P.O. Box 234
          Amenia, NY 12501-0234
Website   http://OrtonAcademy.org
Phone   845-373-8919

Open Court©
Contact   Customer Service
          SRA McGraw-Hill
Address   220 East Danieldale Road
          DeSoto, TX 75115
Website   http://SRAonline.com
Phone   888-772-4543

Project Read/Language Circle©
Contact   Victoria Greene
          Project Read
Address   1629 West 98th Street Suite 130
          Bloomington, MN 55431
Website   http://www.Projectread.com
Phone   952-884-4880

Reading Mastery©
Contact   Customer Service
           SRA McGraw-Hill
Address   220 East Danieldale Road
           DeSoto, TX 75115
Website   http://SRAonline.com
Phone   888-772-4543

Reading Plus©
Contact   Karl Hummel
Address   Taylor and Associates
           110 West Canal St., Suite 301
           Winooski, VT 05404
Website   http://www.readingplus.com
Phone   800-732-3758

Read Well©
Contact   Cambium Learning/Sopris West
Address   4185 Salazar Way
           Frederick, CO 80504
Website   http://www.sopriswest.com
Phone   800-547-6747

Sing, Spell, Read and Write©
Contact   Customer Service Dept.
           Pearson Education
Address   P.O. Box 2500
           145 S. Mount Zion Road
           Lebanon, IN 46052
Website   http://www.pearsonschool.com
Phone   800-848-9500

Sonday System©
Contact   Rich Geist
           Winsor Learning
Address   1620 West 7th Street
           St. Paul, MN 55102
Website   http://SondaySystem.com
Phone   800-321-7585

Spellography©
Contact   Cambium Learning/Sopris West
Address   4185 Salazar Way
           Frederick, CO 80504

Website   http://www.sopriswest.com
Phone   800-547-6747

Success for All©
Contact   Outreach Dept.
          Success For All Foundation
Address   200 W. Towsontown Boulevard
          Baltimore, MD 21204
Website   http://www.successforall.net
Phone   800-548-4998 Ext. 2372

Trophies©
Contact   Customer Service
          Houghton Mifflin Harcourt
Address   222 Berkeley Street
          Boston, MA 02116
Website   http://www.hmhschool.com
Phone   800-225-5425

Voyager Universal Literacy©
Contact   Cambium Learning/Voyager Learning
Address   4185 Salazar Way
          Frederick, CO 80504
Website   http://www.voyagerlearning.com
Phone   800-547-6747

Wilson Reading System©
Contact   Wilson Language Training
Address   47 Old Webster Road
          Oxford, MA 01540
Website   http://www.wilsonlanguage.com
Phone   800-899-8454

FREE PHONICS PRODUCTS

The following are available on the website of the National Right to Read Foundation, www.nrrf.org:

- Blend Phonics
- Phonics Primer
- Reading Competency Test

GRADED READING PASSAGES

Such resources are generally available to teachers and oftentimes are used as a fast tool to verify reading levels without the need to administer a standardized test. One example is the Ekwall/Shanker Reading Inventory, which provides reading-level passages and directions for scoring.

This is available at www.amazon.com/Ekwall-Shanker-Reading Inventory-4th/dp/0205304419.

However, parents and teachers can verify the reading level of any passage by inserting the text into a Word document. To enable this feature, perform the following steps:

1. Under the Word menu, click "Preferences."
2. On the list on the left, click on "Spelling and Grammar."
3. Check the "Show Readability Statistics" box under "Grammar."
4. After inserting text into the document, choose "Spelling and Grammar" under the "Tools" menu. When the program is finished checking, it will display the readability statistics, including the grade level based on the Flesch-Kincade Index.

If this procedure doesn't work for your version of Word, just click on Word "Help" and ask for "Readability Statistics." Then follow the instructions.

The grade level of any document can be ascertained using this function.

See also *Step By Step: A Day-By-Day Programme of Systematic Synthetic Phonics for All Ages*, a British publication by Mona McNee (see pages 136–39). She describes this as a "simple program to teach how to read and spell." The following are her directions for ordering:

Send a $10 bill (not a cheque as they cost too much to convert) and your postal address to:

Mona McNee, M.B.E.
2 Keats Avenue, Whiston
Merseyside, England L35 2XR

Glossary

Alphabetic Principle. The concept that sounds are associated with letters and that those sounds can then be combined to form words.

Automaticity. The ability to engage in an activity without conscious awareness of the individual tasks required to perform it. Automaticity is usually the result of over-learning through repetition and practice. Examples include tying one's shoes, typing on a keyboard, and decoding printed words.

Child-Centric Curriculum. Instructional approaches that appeal to children's specific needs and interests. (In a child-centric classroom, the teacher functions as the facilitator rather than as the dispenser of knowledge.)

Code-Based Instruction. Reading instruction that is based on the alphabetic principle.

Constructivism. A learning theory that emphasizes a student's prior knowledge and experiences as fundamental tools for constructing meaning from text.

Holistic Reading. An approach to reading instruction that stresses the need to view words and text as one integrated whole as opposed to the sum of their individual parts. Whole-Language and other constructivist methods are expressions of holism.

Longitudinal Study. Research that tracks the progress of the same individuals over a specified period of time.

Meta-Analysis. The composite analysis of many studies that examines a specified research topic. Meta-analysis, when properly performed, produces estimates of the viability of a given treatment that are more cogent than those derived from any individual study.

Pedagogy. Another word for teaching or instruction.

Phoneme. The smallest units of speech or sound from which words are comprised. The English language has forty-four phonemes.

Phonemic Awareness. The understanding that letters or letter combinations of an alphabetic language (such as English) represent sounds heard in speech.

Phonics. A strategy for the teaching of reading that emphasizes the relationship between letters and phonemes and the sounds they represent.

The Progressive Movement. A movement that occurred in the early to mid-1900s during which reading instruction began using whole words as the basic unit of instruction, as opposed to analysis of their alphabetic components.

Research Synthesis. The process of compiling and analyzing large quantities of research, and summarizing the aggregate data.

Response to Intervention (RtI). A process that addresses learning problems through the use of research-based practices, continuous progress monitoring, and collaboration among school staff.

SBRR. An acronym for scientifically based reading research, which applies rigorous adherence to empirical methods, including the presence of both treatment and control groups, random assignment to groups, and rigorous analysis of sufficient data to allow an experimenter to make claims relevant to the general population.

Systematic Instruction. Teaching that applies direct and intense measures and follows a sequential pattern as a strategy for skill-building.

Whole-Language. A whole-to-part instructional approach that fosters reading growth by allowing students, from the very beginning, to derive meaning from their every interaction with text.

References

Adams, Gary L., Timothy A. Slocum, Gary L. Railsback, Scott A. Gallagher, Sarah A. McCright, Randy A. Uchytil, William W. Conlon, and James T. Davis. "A Critical Review of Randall Ryder's Report of Direct Instruction Reading in Two Wisconsin School Districts." *Journal of Direct Instruction* 4, no. 2 (Summer 2004): 111–27.

Adams, Marilyn J. *Beginning to Read: Thinking and Learning about Print.* Cambridge, MA: MIT Press, 1990.

Adams, Marilyn Jager, and Maggie Bruck. "Resolving the 'Great Debate.'" *American Educator* 19, no. 2 (Summer 1995): 7, 10–20.

Anderson, Richard C., Elfrieda H. Hiebert, Judith A. Scott, Ian A. G. Wilkinson, with contributions from members of the Commission on Reading. *Becoming a Nation of Readers: The Report of the Commission on Reading.* Washington, DC: The National Institute of Education, U.S. Department of Education, 1985.

Armstrong, Thomas. *In Their Own Way: Discovering and Encouraging Your Child's Personal Learning Style.* New York: Tarcher/Putnam, 1987.

Balmuth, Miriam. *The Roots of Phonics: A Historical Introduction.* New York: McGraw-Hill, 1982.

Berliner, David C. "Educational Research: The Hardest Science of All." *Educational Researcher* 31, no. 8 (2002): 18–20.

Blumenfeld, Samuel. *The New Illiterates: And How to Keep Your Child From Becoming One.* Boise, ID: Paradigm Company, 1988.

Bond, Guy L., and Robert Dykstra. "The Cooperative Research Program in First-Grade Reading Instruction." *Reading Research Quarterly* (Summer 1967): 5–142.

Brooks, Jacqueline Grennon, and Martin G. Brooks. *In Search of Understanding: The Case for Constructivist Classrooms.* Alexandria, VA: Association for Supervision and Curriculum Development, 1999.

Brunner, Michael S. *Retarding America: The Imprisonment of Potential*. Portland, OR: Halcyon House, 1993.

———. "Reduced Recidivism and Increased Employment Opportunity through Research-Based Reading Instruction." Washington, DC: Department of Justice, Office of Juvenile Justice and Delinquency Prevention, 1993.

Calkins, Lucy McCormick, et al. *A Teacher's Guide to Standardized Reading Tests: Knowledge Is Power*. Portsmouth, NH: Heinemann, 1998, p. 51. Quoted in Mike Schmoker, "Radically Redefining Literacy Instruction: An Immense Opportunity." *Phi Delta Kappan* (March 2007): 488–93.

Carbo, Marie. "Debunking the Great Phonics Myth." *Phi Delta Kappan* 70, no. 3 (November 1988): 226–40.

Carey, Kevin. "The Pangloss Index: How States Game the No Child Left Behind Act." *Education Sector*, November 13, 2007.

Chall, Jeanne S. "Afterword." In *Becoming a Nation of Readers: The Report of the Commission on Reading*, by Richard C. Anderson, Elfrieda H. Hiebert, Judith A. Scott, Ian A. G. Wilkinson, with contributions from members of the Commission on Reading. Washington, DC: The National Institute of Education, U.S. Department of Education, 1985.

———. *Learning to Read: The Great Debate*. 3rd ed. Fort Worth, TX: Harcourt Brace, 1996.

Chung, He Len, Michelle Little, Laurence Steinberg, and David Altschuler. "Juvenile Justice and the Transition to Adulthood." *Network on Transitions to Adulthood Policy Brief*, no. 20 (February 2005).

Church, Susan M. *The Future of Whole-Language: Reconstruction or Self-Destruction*. Portsmouth, NH: Heinemann, 1996.

Cooper, Harris M., and Kelle Reach. "What Is a Meta-Analysis and How Do We Know We Can Trust It?" In *The Voice of Evidence: Bringing Research to Classroom Educators*, edited by Peggy McCardle and Vinita Chhabra. Baltimore, MD: Brookes Publishing Company, 2004.

Cordts, Anna D. *Phonics for the Reading Teacher*. New York: Holt, Rinehart and Winston, 1965.

Core Knowledge Foundation, The. coreknowledge.org/.

Covey, Stephen R. *The Seven Habits of Highly Effective People: Restoring the Character Ethic*. New York: Fireside/Simon & Schuster, 1989.

Covey, Stephen R., A. Roger Merrill, and Rebecca R. Merrill. *First Things First*. New York: Fireside/Simon & Schuster, 1994.

Cremin, Lawrence A., ed. *The Republic and the School: Horace Mann on the Education of Free Men (Classics in Education No. 1)*. New York: Teachers College Press, 1957.

Cromwell, Sharon. "Whole-Language and Phonics: Can They Work Together?" Education World, 1997, www.education-world.com/a_curr/curr029.shtml.

Currier, Lillian B. "Phonics or No Phonics?" *Elementary School Journal* (December 1916).

de Lemos, Marion. *Closing the Gap between Research and Practice: Foundations for the Acquisition of Literacy*. Camberwall, Victoria, Australia: ACER Press, 2002.

Diringer, David. *The Alphabet: A Key to the History of Mankind*. 3rd ed., completely revised, with the collaboration of Reinhold Regensburger. 2 vols. London: Hutchinson, 1968.

Dykstra, Robert. "Phonics and Beginning Reading Instruction." In *Teaching Reading: A Phonic/Linguistic Approach to Developmental Reading*, edited by Charles Child Walcutt, Joan Lamport, and Glenn McCracken. New York: Macmillan, 1974.

Farkas, George. *Children of the Code: Television, DVD, and Web Documentary Series*. Personal transcription from video. www.childrenofthecode.org/.

Filler, Louis, ed. *Horace Mann on the Crisis in Education*. Yellow Springs, OH: Antioch Press, 1965.

Finn, Chester E., Jr. Transcript of an interview sponsored by *Education Week*. March 5, 2008.

Flesch, Rudolf. *Why Johnny Can't Read – And What You Can Do About It*. New York: Harper & Brothers, Publishers, 1955.

Fletcher, Jack McFarlin, and G. Reid Lyon. "Reading: A Research-Based Approach." In *What's Gone Wrong in America's Classrooms*, edited by Williamson M. Evers, 49–90. Stanford, CA: Hoover, 1998.

Freepon, P. "Children's Concepts of the Nature and Purpose of Reading in Different Instructional Settings." *Journal of Reading Behavior* 23, no. 2 (1991): 139–63.

Friedman, Thomas L. *The World Is Flat: A Brief History of the Twenty-First Century*. New York: Farrar, Straus & Giroux, 2005.

Fritsma, Teri (sociologist specializing in research methodology and social stratification, and senior project consultant, Minnesota State Colleges and University System). Interview by author. November 11, 2008.

Fuller, Bruce, and Emily Hannum, eds. *Strong States, Weak Schools: The Benefits and Dilemmas of Centralized Accountability*. Bingley, UK: Emerald Group Publishing, Ltd., 2008.

Garrison, S. C., and Minnie Taylor Heard. "An Experimental Study of the Value of Phonetics." *Peabody Journal of Education* 9 (July 1931).

Glaser, Robert. "Foreword." In *Becoming a Nation of Readers: The Report of the Commission on Reading*, by Richard C. Anderson, Elfrieda H. Hiebert, Judith A. Scott, Ian A. G. Wilkinson, with contributions from members of the Commission on Reading. Washington, DC: The National Institute of Education, U.S. Department of Education, 1985.

Goodman, Kenneth S. "Who's Afraid of Whole-Language? Politics, Paradigms, Pedagogy, and the Press." In *In Defense of Good Teaching: What Teachers Need to Know About the "Reading Wars,"* edited by Kenneth S. Goodman. York, ME: Stenhouse Publishers, 1998.

Goodman, Yetta M. "Roots of the Whole-Language Movement." *The Elementary School Journal* (1989).

Government Accountability Office. *Reading First: States Report Improvements in Reading Instruction, but Additional Procedures Would Clarify Education's Role in Ensuring Proper Implementation by States*. GAO-07-161. February 2007.

Greenberg, Elizabeth, Eric Dunleavy, Mark Kutner, and Sheida E. White. *Literacy Behind Bars: Results From the 2003 National Assessment of Adult Literacy Prison Survey*. U.S. Department of Education, Institute of Educational Sciences, National Center for Education Statistics. May 2007.

Haberman, Martin. *Children of the Code: Television, DVD, and Web Documentary Series*. Personal transcription from video. www.childrenofthecode.org/.

Hart, Betty, and Todd Risley. "The Early Catastrophe: The 30 Million Word Gap by Age 3." *American Educator* (Spring 2003). www.aft.org/pubs-reports/american_ educator/spring2003/catastrophe.html.

Herman, Rebecca. *An Educators' Guide to Schoolwide Reform.* American Institutes for Research/Educational Research Service. www.aasa.org/issues_and_ insights/district_organization/Reform/index.htm.

Humboldt Literacy Project. "Fast Facts on Literacy from the National Institute for Literacy." www.eurekawebs.com/humlit/fast_facts.htm.

Klein, Diane Ravitch. "Right on Reading: NYC Schools Finally Get Smart." *New York Post*, September 1, 2008.

Levine, Art. "The Great Debate Revisited." *The Atlantic Online*, December 1994. www.theatlantic.com/politics/education/levine.htm.

Lionni, Paolo, and Lana J. Klass. *The Leipzig Connection: The Systematic Destruction of American Education.* Portland, OR: Heron Books, 1980.

Lucas, Jeff (associate professor and director of graduate studies, Department of Sociology, University of Maryland). In telephone conference with the author. July 22, 2008.

Lyon, G. Reid. *Children of the Code: Television, DVD, and Web Documentary Series.* www.childrenofthecode.org/interviews/lyon.htm.

Mann, Horace. *Lectures and Annual Reports on Education.* Cambridge, MA: The Editor, 1867.

Manzo, Kathleen Kennedy. "Study Challenges Direct Reading Method." *Education Week* (January 28, 2004).

Marsden, George M. *Jonathan Edwards: A Life.* New Haven, CT: Yale University Press, 2003.

McNee, Mona, and Alice Coleman. *The Great Reading Disaster: Reclaiming Our Educational Birthright.* Charlottesville, VA: Imprint Academic Philosophy Documentation Center, 2007.

McNee, Mona. Posting on Reading and Reading Disabilities Group. July 19, 2008. groups.yahoo.com/group/readbygrade3/.

———. Posting on Reading and Reading Disabilities Group. June 10, 2008. groups. yahoo.com/group/readbygrade3/.

———. *Step By Step: A Day-by-Day Programme of Systematic, Synthetic Phonics for All Ages,* rev. ed. Merseyside, England: Mona McNee, 2008.

Messerli, Jonathan. *Horace Mann: A Biography.* New York: Knopf, 1972.

Moats, Louisa. *Children of the Code: Television, DVD, and Web Documentary Series.* Personal transcription from video. www.childrenofthecode.org/.

———. *Whole-Language Lives On: The Illusion of "Balanced" Reading Instruction.* Washington, DC: Thomas B. Fordham Foundation, 2000.

Monaghan, E. Jennifer. "Phonics and Whole Word/Whole-Language Controversies, 1948–1998: An Introductory History." In *Finding Our Literacy Roots: Eighteenth Yearbook of the American Reading Forum,* edited by Richard J. Telfer, 1–23. Whitewater, WI: American Reading Forum, 1998.

Moretti, Enrico. "Crime and the Costs of Criminal Justice." In *The Price We Pay: Economic and Social Consequences of Inadequate Education,* ed. Clive Belfield and Henry M. Levin. Washington, DC: Brookings, 2007.

Mosher, Raymond M., and Sidney M. Newhall. "Phonic Versus Look-and-Say Training in Beginning Reading." *Journal of Educational Psychology* 21 (October 1930).

Moustafa, Margaret. *Beyond Traditional Phonics*. Portsmouth, NH: Heinemann, 1997.

Nation's Report Card, The. "Reading 2007 State Snapshot Report, Alabama." U. S. Department of Education, Institute of Education Sciences, National Center for Education Statistics. nces.ed.gov/pubSearch/pubsinfo.asp?pubid=2007496.

———. "Reading 2007 State Snapshot Report, Massachusetts." U. S. Department of Education, Institute of Education Sciences, National Center for Education Statistics. nces.ed.gov/pubSearch/pubsinfo.asp?pubid=2007496.

National Assessment of Adult Literacy. U. S. Department of Education, Institute of Education Sciences, National Center for Education Statistics. nces.ed.gov/naal/.

National Assessment of Educational Progress, 2007 Report on Reading. nationsreportcard.gov/reading_2007/.

National Commission on Excellence in Education, The. *An Open Letter to the American People: A Nation at Risk: The Imperative for Educational Reform* (April 1983). www.ed.gov/pubs/NatAtRisk/index.html.

National Early Literacy Panel. *Developing Early Literacy: Report of the National Early Literacy Panel: A Scientific Synthesis of Early Literacy Development and Implications for Intervention*. Jessup, MD: National Institute for Literacy, 2008. www.nifl.gov/nifl/publications/pdf/NELPReport09.pdf.

National Reading Panel. *Teaching Children to Read: An Evidence-Based Assessment of the Scientific Research Literature on Reading and Its Implications for Reading Instruction: Reports of the Subgroups*. April 2000. www.nichd.nih.gov/publications/nrp/report.cfm.

Paul, Richard, and Linda Elder. *A Critical Thinker's Guide to Educational Glitz and Glitter*. Dillon Beach, CA: Foundation for Critical Thinking, 2007.

Pearson, P. David. "Foreword." In *Beginning to Read: Thinking and Learning about Print*, by Marilyn J. Adams, v–viii. Cambridge, MA: MIT Press, 1990.

Pfeffer, Jeffrey, and Robert I. Sutton. *The Knowing-Doing Gap: How Smart Companies Turn Knowledge into Action*. Boston, MA: Harvard Business School Press, 2000.

Pflaum, Susanna W., Herbert J. Walberg, Myra L. Karegianes, and Sue P. Rasher. "Reading Instruction: A Quantitative Analysis." *Educational Researcher* (July–August 1980): 12–18.

Pressley, Michael. "A Few Things Reading Educators Should Know about Instructional Experiments." *The Reading Teacher* 57, no. 1 (September 2003): 64–71.

Reschly, Daniel J., Lynn R. Holdheide, Susan M. Smartt, and Regina M. Oliver, *Evaluation of LBS-I Teacher Preparation in Inclusive Practices, Reading and Classroom Organization-Behavior Management*. Springfield: Illinois State Board of Education, 2008.

Reutzel, D. Ray, and Robert B. Cooter. "Whole-Language: Comparative Effects on First-Grade Reading Achievement." *Journal of Educational Research* 83, no. 5 (May–June 1990): 252–57.

Rhodes, Lynn K. "Comprehension and Predictability: An Analysis of Beginning Reading Materials." In *New Perspectives on Comprehension: Monographs in*

Teaching and Learning Number 3, edited by Jerome C. Harste and Robert F. Carey. Bloomington, IN: Indiana University School of Education, 1979.

Ribowsky, Helene. "The Comparative Effects of a Code Emphasis Approach and a Whole-Language Approach upon Emergent Literacy of Kindergarten Children." PhD. diss., New York University, 1986.

Russell, David H. "A Diagnostic Study of Spelling Readiness." *Journal of Educational Research* 37 (December 1943): 276–83.

Ryder, Randall J., Jen L. Sekulski, and Anna Silberg. "Results of Direct Instruction Reading Program Evaluation Longitudinal Results: First Through Third Grade, 2000–2003. www.uwm.edu/News/PR/04.01/DI_Final_Report_2003.pdf.

Sawchuk, Stephen. "Leadership Gap Seen in Post-NCLB Changes in U.S. Teachers." *Education Week* 28, no. 3 (September 10, 2008): 1, 16.

Schaefer, Ed. *Creating World Class Schools: Peak Performance through Direct Instruction* (Presentation Notebook), 2000.

Seuss, Dr. *Dr. Seuss's ABC*. New York: Random House, 1991. First published in 1963.

Sexton, Elmer K., and John S. Herron. "The Newark Phonics Experiment." *Elementary School Journal* 28 (May 1928): 690–701.

Shanahan, Timothy. *Children of the Code: Television, DVD, and Web Documentary Series*. Personal transcription from video. www.childrenofthecode.org/.

Shavelson, Richard J., and Lisa Towne, eds. *Scientific Research in Education*. Washington, DC: Committee on Scientific Principles for Education Research, Center for Education, Division of Behavioral and Social Sciences and Education, National Research Council, National Academy Press, 2002.

Shaywitz, Sally. *Overcoming Dyslexia: A New and Complete Science-Based Program for Reading Problems at Any Level*. New York: Random House, 2003.

Sherman, Lawrence W., and Richard A. Berk. "The Minneapolis Domestic Violence Experiment." *Police Foundation Reports* 1 (1984): 1–8.

———. "The Specific Deterrent Effects of Arrest for Domestic Assault." *American Sociological Review* 49, no. 2 (April 1984): 261–72.

Simmons, Deborah C., et al. "Translating Research into Basal Reading Programs: Applications of Curriculum Design." *LD Forum* 20, no. 1 (Fall 1994): 9–13.

Smith, Frank. "The Just So Story—Obvious But False." In *Unspeakable Acts, Unnatural Practices: Flaws and Fallacies in "Scientific" Reading Instruction*, by Frank Smith, 40–44. Portsmouth, NH: Heinemann, 2003. [Based on the article "The Just So Story—Obvious But False," in *Language Arts* 80, 4.]

———. *Unspeakable Acts, Unnatural Practices: Flaws and Fallacies in "Scientific" Reading Instruction*. Portsmouth, NH: Heinemann, 2003.

Smith, Nila Banton. *American Reading Instruction: Its Development and Its Significance in Gaining a Perspective on Current Practices in Reading*. New York: Silver, Burdett and Company, 1934.

Snow, Catherine E., M. Susan Burns, and Peg Griffin, eds. *Preventing Reading Difficulties in Young Children*. Washington, DC: National Academy Press, 1998.

Stager, Gary S. "Meet Frank Smith: Gifts of Wisdom for Educators." *District Administration Magazine* (December 2003).

Stern, Sol. *Too Good to Last: The True Story of Reading First*. Washington, DC: Thomas B. Fordham Foundation, March 2008.

Stone, J. E. "Learning Requires More Than Play," *Education Matters* (August 2004): 2, 7. www.education-consumers.org/JES_EdMatters_0804.pdf.

Sweet, Robert W. Jr. "Illiteracy: An Incurable Disease or Education Malpractice?" The National Right to Read Foundation (1996). www.nrrf.org/essay_Illiteracy. html.

Tedrow, Mary. "Are American Public Schools Inherently Biased?" *Teacher Magazine*, July 16, 2008.

U.S. Department of Education. *The Reading Excellence Act* (Archived Information). www.ed.gov/inits/FY99/1-read.html.

Walsh, Kate, Deborah Glaser, and Danielle Dunne Wilcox. *What Education Schools Aren't Teaching about Reading and What Elementary Teachers Aren't Learning, Executive Summary*. Washington, DC: National Council on Teacher Quality, May 2006 (Revised January 2007).

Wendorf, James. *Children of the Code: Television, DVD, and Web Documentary Series.* www.childrenofthecode.org/interviews/wendorf.htm.

What Works Clearinghouse. *Intervention: Reading Mastery, August 2008.* U.S. Department of Education, Institute of Education Sciences. ies.ed.gov/ncee/wwc/pdf/WWC_ReadingMastery_081208.pdf.

Whitehurst, Grover (Russ). *Children of the Code: Television, DVD, and Web Documentary Series.* www.childrenofthecode.org/interviews/whitehurst.htm.

Wonder of Reading, The. "The Library Crisis." www.wonderofreading.org/statistics.htm.

Zorza, Joan. 1992. "The Criminal Law of Misdemeanor Domestic Violence, 1970–90." *Journal of Criminal Law and Criminology* 83: 46–72.

Index

ability groupings, appropriate use of, 141

academic learning time, Direct Instruction and, 109–10

Adams, Gary, 70, 76n9

Adams, Marilyn Jager, 35, 38, 40–42, 48n5, 48n7, 49n14, 49n20

affective instructional models, effectiveness of, 37

age-appropriate reading proficiency: Direct Instruction and, 15; guaranteeing, 127

aggressive behavior, illiteracy and, 81–82, 123

Agnew, Donald C., 27–28

Alexander, Duane, 10

alphabetic principle: construction of meaning and, 2–3, 40; constructivism and, 3, 21; early American use of, 22–23, 135–36; early literacy and, 8, 47–48; effective use of, 39–40; glossary entry for, 157; guaranteeing mastery of, 135–36; historical opposition to, 22–25; holism and, 52; ideological opposition to, 52–53, 65–66; reading comprehension and, 66; scientific support for, 8, 33, 35, 37–38, 39–42, 44–47

Anderson, Richard, 38–40, 49n15, 49nn17–18

antisocial behavior, illiteracy and, 81–82

automaticity, 41, 141; glossary entry for, 157

"Balanced Literacy," 69, 99

basal programs, effectiveness of, 35, 111

basic skills instructional models. *See* alphabetic principle; code-based instruction; Direct Instruction; phonics instruction; systematic instruction

Becoming a Nation of Readers, 32, 38–40, 49nn15–17, 90–91

Beginning to Read: Thinking and Learning about Print, 40–42, 48n5, 49n7, 49n14, 49n20

behavior management, Direct Instruction and, 112–13

Berk, Richard, 57

Bisek, Doris, 117n3

Blachman, Benita, 10

incarcerated students, 83–85
incarceration, illiteracy and, 78, 81–85
ideology: as barrier to progress,
    145–46; constructivism and, 65–66;
    opposition to alphabetic principle
    and, 52, 65–66; reading failure and,
    142; reading instruction driven
    by, 90–91, 94–95; reading science
    and, 52, 66–67; whole language
    instruction and, 65–66
illiteracy: academic consequences
    of, 120–26; aggression and,
    81–82; democracy and, 79–80;
    discrimination and, 79–81;
    employment and, 78; eradication
    of, 136; as failure of educational
    establishment, 77; healthcare and,
    79; incarceration and, 78, 81–85;
    need for different approach to,
    85–87; placing of blame for, 126–28;
    as public health crisis, 10, 22, 42, 57,
    134; school failure and, 30; scientific
    explanation of, 10; social costs
    of, 78–82, 119–20, 121–25; social
    isolation and, 81; social justice and,
    80–81; whole-language instruction
    and, 29
individuality, student: experimental
    science and, 56–57
innovation in reading practice, 97–106
instructional time, effective use of,
    109–10
interventions, 14, 15, 142–43, 144

Karegianes, 37–38, 50nn12–13
Keillor, Garrison, syndicated column
    of, 59–60
kindergarteners, reading readiness in,
    39, 47

Laboratory School, University of
    Chicago, 26
language acquisition, critical period
    for, 142–43
Learning to Read: The Great Debate,
    32–34, 37, 48n4, 49n18, 49n22
learning time, effective use of, 109–10

Le Floch, Kerstin, 99
legislation: No Child Left Behind
    Act, 44, 59–60, 68–75; Reading
    Excellence Act, 67
letters, ability to name, 47
literacy coaches, Direct Instruction
    and, 116
longitudinal studies, 70; glossary
    entry for, 157
low socio-economic status, students
    of: reading failure and, 15, 120–25;
    reading instruction and, 4, 33–34
Lucas, Jeff, 55–56, 63n3
Lyon, G. Reid, interview with, 93–95

Mann, Horace, 22–25, 28nn5–9
McNee, Mona, case of, 136–39,
    144nn6–7
meaning-based instruction. *See*
    constructivism; holism; whole
    language instruction
meaning construction: alphabetic
    principle and, 2–3, 40; automaticity
    and, 41; decoding ability and, 111–
    12; importance to reading ability of,
    29–30, 33–34; phonics instruction
    and, 9
meta-analysis: glossary entry for, 157;
    major studies involving, 32–48
minorities: Direct Instruction and, 112;
    illiteracy and, 80–81, 82
motivation, drill-based instruction
    and, 140–41

National Council on Teacher Quality,
    18, 61, 91–93
National Early Literacy Panel, 47–48,
    49nn39–43
National Institute for Literacy, 47
National Reading Panel, 44, 49nn25–38
New Illiterates, The, 36, 48n10
No Child Left Behind Act: alleged
    underfunding of, 71; circumventing
    of, 72–75; Garrison Keillor's
    syndicated column on, 59–60;
    politicization of, 68; Reading First
    and, 72–74; reading research and,

About the Author

Anthony Pedriana has been telling his story and bringing the message of his research to numerous school groups and literacy organizations across the country. Prior to that he had spent thirty-five years in the Milwaukee Public Schools serving in various capacities, including teacher, principal and mentor to principals. He currently resides with his wife, Mary Jo, in River Falls, Wisconsin.